Advance praise f
Incubators of Innovation

"Today's students are faced with an uncertain future where the guarantees of secure employment seem a distant dream. To meet these challenges, colleges need to prepare students with the tools to help them craft their own future by developing an entrepreneurial mindset that makes them independent, self-motivated problem-solvers for the twenty-first century. As this book demonstrates, the National Association for Community College Entrepreneurship (NACCE) has been a leader in encouraging this transformation within community colleges. This book provides a practical guide with many examples that encourage entrepreneurial thinking among students and within institutions. I hope you find the book a compelling call to action within your own organization."

—***Desh Deshpande***, *Founder, Deshpande Foundation; Life Member, MIT Corporation; Entrepreneur; and Author,* On Entrepreneurship and Impact

"Entrepreneurial thinking has the power to facilitate transformational change within our colleges, and this book captures the essence of not only how it can but also why it should. Whether energizing educators to seek innovative curriculum designs or creating partnerships to better address complex workforce issues in the twenty-first century, the contributors make it clear that the entrepreneurial college is the new standard of excellence."

—***Edwin Massey***, *President, Indian River State College; Fort Pierce, Florida*

"Community colleges have always been the 'go-to' place that enables people at all ages and stages of development to access the knowledge and skills needed for work and play. I started my educational path at a community college. Community colleges attract instructors with deep expertise, many of whom have been extremely successful in the private sector. In addition to being subject-matter experts, they are great teachers who are willing to share their knowledge and experience with others. This book reflects this commitment. The contributors, who have brought significant benefits to their communities, are now sharing their knowledge and insights with those of us who seek new knowledge and new ways of improving our practice. We applaud NACCE's leadership in bringing these contributors together to provide this new resource for invention educators who must blend making, inventing, and entrepreneurship together as they prepare the next generation of innovators."

—**Stephanie Couch**, *Executive Director, Lemelson-MIT Program*

"Educating the next generation of entrepreneurs is rapidly and rightfully becoming a primary focus of institutions of higher education around the globe. In this book, Corbin and Thomas have masterfully assembled a range of impactful, original, and dynamic entrepreneurship education leaders from across the United States to talk insightfully about best practices in our community college system that are sure to spur entrepreneurial action both on and off campus for years to come."

—**Eric Liguori**, *Rohrer Chair for Entrepreneurship, Rowan University; President, United States Association for Small Business and Entrepreneurship*

"With the economy transforming at an increasing pace, it is essential that communities continue to empower institutions that will provide the leadership that keeps them connected and competitive. Community colleges are that key institution for many communities around the country, and the authors of *Community Colleges as Incubators of Innovation* take another step in providing that leadership. The clear examples, tools, and lessons gained from their experiences offer insights that can help make any organization entrepreneurial as communities adapt to the changing economy of the twenty-first century."

—**Tim Shaw**, *Senior Policy Analyst, Bipartisan Policy Center*

"Our nation's system of community colleges is a vital resource, and I'd urge anyone concerned about the future of our country to read *Community Colleges as Incubators of Innovation*. This book offers a tapestry of case studies describing the inspiring innovations of community colleges that are determined to equip students of all ages with the 'entrepreneurial-ness' needed in careers spanning business, academia, public policy, or social services. As these community colleges reimagine their role, they are leading the way in providing students with compelling and cost-effective paths to fulfilling lives in an oh-so-dynamic world."

—**Ted Dintersmith**, *Author*, What School Could Be

COMMUNITY COLLEGES AS
INCUBATORS OF INNOVATION

Series Editors: Angela Long and Susan Slesinger

Also in the Innovative Ideas for Community Colleges series:

Overcoming Educational Racism in the Community College: Creating Pathways to Success for Minority and Impoverished Student Populations
 Edited by Angela Long
 Foreword by Walter G. Bumphus

COMMUNITY COLLEGES AS INCUBATORS OF INNOVATION

Unleashing Entrepreneurial Opportunities for Communities and Students

Edited by

Rebecca A. Corbin and Ron Thomas

Foreword by Andy Stoll

Afterword by J. Noah Brown

STERLING, VIRGINIA

Published by Stylus Publishing, LLC.
22883 Quicksilver Drive
Sterling, Virginia 20166-2012

Library of Congress Cataloging-in-Publication Data
Names: Corbin, Rebecca A., editor. | Thomas, Ron (Ronald E.), editor.
Title: Community colleges as incubtors of innovation : unleashing
    opportunities for communities and students / edited by Rebecca A. Corbin
    and Ron Thomas ; foreword by Andy Stoll afterword by J. Noah Brown.
Description: First edition. | Sterling, Virginia : Stylus Publishing, LLC.,
    2019. | Series: Innovative ideas for community colleges series | Includes
    bibliographical references and index.
Identifiers: LCCN 2018033998 (print) | LCCN 2018055483 (ebook) |
    ISBN 9781620368657 (ePub, mobi) | ISBN 9781620368640 (uPDF) |
    ISBN 9781620368626 (cloth : acid-free paper) | ISBN 9781620368633
    (paperback : acid-free paper) | ISBN 9781620368640 (library networkable
    e-edition) | ISBN 9781620368657 (consumer e-edition)
Subjects: LCSH: Community colleges--Curricula--United States. |
    Community colleges--Administration--United States. |
    Entrepreneurship--Study and teaching (Higher)--United States. |
    Community and college--United States.
Classification: LCC LB2328 (ebook) | LCC LB2328 .M25 2019 (print) |
    DDC 378.1/5430973--dc23
LC record available at https://lccn.loc.gov/2018033998

13-digit ISBN: 978-1-62036-862-6 (cloth)
13-digit ISBN: 978-1-62036-863-3 (paperback)
13-digit ISBN: 978-1-62036-864-0 (library networkable e-edition)
13-digit ISBN: 978-1-62036-865-7 (consumer e-edition)

Printed in the United States of America

All first editions printed on acid-free paper
that meets the American National Standards Institute
Z39-48 Standard.

Bulk Purchases
Quantity discounts are available for use in workshops and
for staff development.
Call 1-800-232-0223

First Edition, 2019

*To Andy Scibelli and all of the entrepreneurs
who believed in and supported this idea.*

CONTENTS

FOREWORD

All of the money in the world cannot solve problems unless we work together. And if we work together, there is no problem in the world that can stop us, as we seek to develop people to their highest potential.

— Ewing Marion Kauffman

When Ewing Marion Kauffman launched Marion Labs in his Kansas City basement in 1950, with just $5,000 and a dream, he could not have known the lasting impact he'd have on the world. Over the course of the years to come, he'd grow a billion-dollar company, establish one of the best-performing stocks of the era, create jobs for thousands of people, improve the livelihoods of thousands more, and launch the Ewing Marion Kauffman Foundation in his name. The Kauffman Foundation is built on a legacy that epitomizes the entrepreneurial spirit it has championed for nearly three decades.

The Kauffman Foundation's research over the last three decades has borne out much of what Mr. Kauffman knew intuitively—that two of the most powerful forces that can lift up both individuals and their communities are a high-quality education and the opportunity to become an entrepreneur. Entrepreneurship matters to our communities. It empowers individuals; improves standards of living; and contributes jobs, wealth, and innovation to the economy. In fact, new and young companies—started by entrepreneurs—create most of the net new jobs in the United States.

It is in this spirit that this pioneering book comes together, a modern take on the intertwining forces of education and entrepreneurship through the lens of the community college. This book is about what it takes to lead a forward-facing, twenty-first-century community college, one that fully embraces its potential as an educational institution, community leader, convener, connector, and engine of economic growth.

While *entrepreneurial ecosystem building* is a term that has only recently come into wider use, it is a field that has been emerging over the past few decades, led by innovators and pioneers like the National Association for Community College Entrepreneurship (NACCE) and the contributors featured in this book. Ecosystem building reminds us that helping entrepreneurs isn't just about building more incubators, finding more capital, or creating more entrepreneurial training. It's more than that. It's about how we get these ecosystems to work better together across our communities.

Many communities have the elements of an entrepreneurial ecosystem, but they remain nascent or disconnected. The networks may be small, siloed, or fragmented, and their culture may lack vibrancy, trust, and social cohesion. Where such gaps exist, leaders must consider the whole ecosystem while enhancing each of its elements. This book's mission, as envisioned by NACCE leadership, is to help community college leaders and supporters build effective ecosystems in their communities. Ecosystem building is about connecting, empowering, and collaborating with others to build the whole system of support for entrepreneurs, not just that which resides inside one institution or another.

At their core, entrepreneurial ecosystems are based on human relationships. They help create invisible infrastructures to support entrepreneurs. Unlike traditional infrastructure, this is not about physical spaces, fancy buildings, or pools of capital. Instead, entrepreneurial ecosystem building focuses on forging consistent and collaborative human engagement to lift up individuals in communities to pursue their dreams.

In this book, readers will find insights into the role of community colleges in building such ecosystems. Entrepreneurial ecosystem building is an emerging model for economic development, and it will take early adopters to help fully realize its potential in communities everywhere. I firmly believe that community colleges are uniquely positioned to lead the way in helping to build a more resilient, vibrant, inclusive, and entrepreneurial-led economy.

In the early 1930s when Mr. Kauffman enrolled at Kansas City Junior College (now Metropolitan Community College), he couldn't have known the impact of his education and what was in store for his life ahead. Mr. Kauffman believed that everyone has a fundamental right to turn an idea into an economic reality. He saw building enterprise as one of the most effective ways to realize individual promise and spur the economy. It doesn't matter who people are or where they are from. Everyone should face zero barriers along the way. It is only through collective help and support that we can clear the path for these entrepreneurs—the makers, the doers, the dreamers in communities everywhere.

We know entrepreneurial leaders are out there, fighting for entrepreneurs in the trenches, taking actions big and small, day in and day out, whether anyone notices or not. We thank them for everything they do and applaud them for making a real difference.

Andy Stoll
Senior Program Officer in Entrepreneurship
Ecosystem Development and Measurement
Ewing Marion Kauffman Foundation

ACKNOWLEDGMENTS

The entrepreneurial journey is filled with challenges, victories, failures, and life lessons. In writing this book, the authors, along with the National Association for Community College Entrepreneurship (NACCE) community and its network, sought to find meaningful examples of replicable entrepreneurial practices and engagement from college presidents, educators, philanthropists, industry leaders, and government officials. We invited many innovative friends from throughout the country and our community college ecosystem to help us tell the story.

Members of the NACCE board of directors, including Susan May, board chair and president of Fox Valley Technical College; Eugene Giovannini, immediate past chair and chancellor of the Tarrant County College District; Steve Schulz, treasurer/secretary and president of North Iowa Area Community College; and Ed Massey, former board chair and president of Indian River State College, provided guidance and encouragement during NACCE's leadership transition in 2015. Their faith in the entrepreneurial process and belief in a member-serving-member model led to NACCE establishing new and robust relationships with the Michelson 20 MM Foundation; the Verizon Foundation; Verizon Innovative Learning; the U.S. Department of Agriculture–Rural Development; California Community Colleges Doing What MATTERS; the Entrepreneurial Learning Initiative (ELI); Bellevue University; Institute for International Business; and Intuit, and deepening partnerships with the Appalachian Regional Commission (ARC), Burton D. Morgan Foundation, HP Life Foundation, and the Direct Selling Educational Foundation.

In the past several years, NACCE's collaborations with aligned organizations, including the American Association of Community Colleges, Association of Community College Trustees, EntreEd, Ewing Marion Kauffman Foundation, Global MindED, National Institute for Staff and Organizational Development (NISOD), the League for Innovation, U.S. Association for Small Business and Entrepreneurship, and the U.S. Fab Lab Network, helped NACCE to expand our network, amplify our messages, and expand our thought leadership. We thank these people and organizations for donating their time and sharing their stories and advice in an effort to help unleash the entrepreneurial spirit on more community college campuses.

We also recognize the valuable contributions of S. Prestley Blake and NACCE's founding members and staff, as well as Michael Hennessy, president and CEO of the Coleman Foundation, who worked diligently to create a new organization with a laser focus on promoting entrepreneurship in community college classrooms, campuses, and local ecosystems. Many of them are highlighted in the introduction. Several have been officially inducted onto the NACCE Emeritus Advisory committee, including Gail Carberry, Angeline Godwin, Jim Jacobs, and Ron Thomas.

All royalties from this book will be directed to a scholarship fund for professional development in entrepreneurship training for community college faculty and staff.

Rebecca A. Corbin
President and CEO
National Association for Community College Entrepreneurship (NACCE)

Ron Thomas
President (ret.)
NACCE Emeritus Advisory Committee
Dakota County Technical College

THE IMPETUS FOR ENTREPRENEURIAL EDUCATION

Rebecca A. Corbin and Ron Thomas

This global competitive environment demands a more diversified approach to economic development, increasing the relative importance of supporting existing small businesses and entrepreneurs and establishing the conditions under which innovative, entrepreneurial endeavors can take root and grow. These "grow your own" strategies have received increasing attention in recent years as communities, regions and states experiment with new types of policies to support entrepreneurs and small business owners.

—Deborah Markley and Brian Dabson, Rural Policy
Research Institute, Iowa City, Iowa

This book is a chorus of many voices with ideas and guidance to help college leaders engage more effectively with others to help individuals, communities, and colleges prosper. Our goal is to help prepare college leaders to work in an entrepreneurial ecosystem that is fueled by the Internet and a connection economy. This introduction sets the table for how this entrepreneurial journey has evolved and what college leaders can do to take entrepreneurship to the next levels in their communities. It also gives context to the role the National Association for Community College Entrepreneurship (NACCE) has played along the way and continues to play on a national and—more recently—global level. Most of all, it illuminates the creative thinking and bold action that entrepreneurially minded pioneers have taken to meet challenges and embrace change.

Entrepreneurship was the new norm in the 1990s. Spurred by the dawn of the digital age, the economy was booming and household incomes were growing. Communities wanted to capitalize on that growth, and universities across the country were starting entrepreneurship programs on their campuses. An increasing number of students enrolled in higher education, and new businesses launched across the country. In 1994 the Bureau of Labor Statistics reported 500,000 new businesses were founded, growing to 675,000 by 2000. In 1994, those businesses created 4.1 million jobs and, by

2000, that number grew to 4.6 million. Entrepreneurship was the spring-board for making new ideas happen, and relationships between education and businesses served as catalysts for launching many of these start-ups.

While the 1990s were characterized as a decade of opportunity and growth, the decade from 2000 to 2010 was very different. Community college enrollment grew, and by 2009 the recession hit. Unemployment neared 10%, the housing market crashed, and state budgets—including support for higher education—plummeted.

The country was beginning to experience economic uncertainty, and community colleges were positioned to provide another option for people searching for new careers.

At the same time, community college presidents were asked to reduce budgets and educate more and more diverse students while meeting higher accountability standards. Community college leaders needed to do more with less.

The American Association of Community Colleges (AACC) was concerned about the leadership crisis of two-year institutions. One concern was how to prepare new and senior leadership for these challenges; another concern was the waning numbers of professionals prepared for community college leadership. The AACC attempted to address the training needs by organizing workshops, seminars, and dialogues with community college leaders. The White House was promoting community colleges and entrepreneurship opportunities to facilitate positive change in the country. Still, community college presidents were searching for answers to address the growing challenges in community colleges. A new leadership model was needed.

Fortunately, a new organization was already in place that could help address these issues and provide community college leaders and faculty with resources and platforms to help them lay the groundwork for supporting entrepreneurial growth within their communities. In 2002, NACCE was founded at Springfield Technical Community College in Springfield, Massachusetts.

With support from key foundations, private sources, and public entities, NACCE and its founding members believed the organization could serve as a resource to support entrepreneurial teaching and leadership across disciplines and communities. This work has never been more important than it is today and was the impetus for writing this book. Community colleges exploring their place in their ecosystems will find it a fascinating journey—untethered and unpredictable—but not without reward.

Throughout this book, contributors share their experiences and perspectives, providing vital glimpses into the way entrepreneurial thinking and action impact real-world ecosystems. You will read about how college leaders use tools like effectuation, ecosystem mapping, and NACCE's *Presidents for Entrepreneurship Pledge* to meet challenges at hand and explore untapped opportunity. By illustrating how various college and community leaders throughout the country have approached this journey, we hope to bring fresh energy and vigor to those who are at the threshold of creating entrepreneurial ecosystems at their community colleges.

LEADING WITH AN ENTREPRENEURIAL MINDSET

Bree Langemo

This chapter will emphasize the ever-pressing need for community colleges to prioritize entrepreneurship in order to remain relevant, as well as produce the entrepreneurial graduates needed for the future of society. To do so, an entrepreneurial education must be offered broadly and across all disciplines. The chapter will also (a) redefine entrepreneurship in a way that is relevant and broadly accessible, (b) define the key constructs behind the entrepreneurial mindset, and (c) describe how to create entrepreneurial learning environments. Community colleges are uniquely positioned to lead with an entrepreneurial mindset, developing the entrepreneurial workforce needed to overcome the challenges presented by the Fourth Industrial Revolution and the future of work.

The World Is Changing

The world is changing in ways we could have never anticipated. Unlike the industrial revolutions of the past, the Fourth Industrial Revolution is advancing at a far greater pace than humankind has ever experienced. Given the advancement of technology, the new world of work, and changing job types that will require new skill sets, the need for *all levels* of society to be entrepreneurial has never been greater. Yet, our current educational models have not kept pace, with many schools keeping entrepreneurship at the perimeter of their course offerings and academic mindset. It will require significant entrepreneurial leadership to reinvent the current educational model and create the entrepreneurial learning environments needed to cultivate an entrepreneurial mindset in academic leaders, faculty, and students in classrooms and across campuses. The challenge before us is great, and the need to take action is now.

The Fourth Industrial Revolution

The Fourth Industrial Revolution is well underway and is transforming the ways in which we live and work. While the First and Second Industrial Revolutions moved from water and steam power to electrical power to drive production, the Third Industrial Revolution used technology to automate production (Schwab, 2016). Unlike previous industrial revolutions, the Fourth Industrial Revolution emerged at an exponential pace by fusing technologies to transform entire systems of production in nearly every industry. The technological advances in robotics, artificial intelligence, nanotechnology, biotechnology, and many other fields are greatly amplified by how they build on one another (Schwab, 2016).

This technological revolution has and will disrupt employment, leading to the loss of millions of jobs in the global workforce and the evolution of jobs as we know it (World Economic Forum, 2016b). Remarkably, many high demand occupations of today did not exist 5 to 10 years ago (World Economic Forum, 2016b). The World Economic Forum reports how a popular estimate projects "65 percent of children entering primary school today will ultimately end up working in completely new job types that don't yet exist" (2016b, p. 1). The report goes on to detail how the rapidly changing employment pattern presents significant challenges in understanding and developing future skills needed to succeed in the workplace. The speed and scope of change of the Fourth Industrial Revolution, not only in breadth but also in depth, is *unprecedented*, significantly impacting job types, skill sets, and the way we live and work.

The New World of Work

As existing occupations evolve and new occupations come into existence, core skill sets for work will rapidly change. For example, as robotics and machines automate work, workers will be freed up to take on new tasks that require new skill sets (World Economic Forum, 2016b). The high demand skills of the near future simply are not critical to work today (World Economic Forum, 2016b), resulting in a skills gap between today's workforce and the workforce of the future (World Economic Forum & BVL International, 2017).

The World Economic Forum (2017) anticipates that future workforce skills will focus on leadership, strategic and critical thinking, collaboration, problem-solving, and creativity over technical skills. CareerBuilder's (2014) market research supports this trend, finding that 77% of employers indicated that candidates who are self-motivated, collaborative, flexible, effective communicators and problem-solvers have soft skills that are *as important* as the technical skills they may possess. The report further details how 16% of employers indicated that soft skills are actually *more important* than technical skills. Recognizing this heightening attention to soft skills, the World Economic Forum (2017) identifies a challenge in our current educational systems that tends to push students into selecting career paths at an early age, often developing a single technical skill set that pigeonholes graduates into an area of expertise that may or may not create value in the future, while failing to provide them with the noncognitive skills that will help them adapt.

In addition, a new world of work has emerged from the advancement of digitization and Internet connectivity, and work is becoming more independent, self-directed, and flexible with a focus on creating value by solving problems for others. By recent estimates, the new *gig economy* (loosely defined as self-employed work made up of project-based gigs) is made up of millions of U.S. workers comprising around 34% of the current workforce with expectations of significant growth in the coming years (Gillespie, 2017). In addition, more than 80% of corporations are predicted to increase the adoption of a flexible workforce to meet their needs and create value in their organizations (Emergent Research & Intuit Inc., 2010).

Traditional careers and the way we work are rapidly becoming redefined in light of the Fourth Industrial Revolution, yet how we prepare students and what we expect of our graduates has seen little change. Herein lies a mismatch between our methods of preparation and our expectations of graduates, who will be required to create value no matter the discipline they choose and whether or not they find a job at an existing organization in their field of choice, create their own job, or work as an independent contractor. Preparing students for traditional careers and pathways is a disservice not only to their future but also to the future of society, given the ambiguous job types of the future and the evolution of careers and work as we know it. Thus, a renewed focus on how we are developing our human capital for the future of society must be examined.

A New Educational Model

To find a place in the future workforce, graduates will need to align their interests, skills, and abilities with the needs of others to *create value*, whether they work for an employer of an existing organization, start something new, or participate as an independent contractor in the gig economy. This will require graduates to be entrepreneurial, no matter their chosen path or discipline. This will also require educational systems to produce not just entrepreneurs, but rather "entrepreneur-*ials*" with the behavioral and non-cognitive skills needed to adapt and create value in this new world of work.

While educational systems have traditionally focused on ensuring students secure employment upon graduation, it is increasingly more critical that they prepare students for the dynamic, entrepreneurial environments that they will inevitably enter (World Economic Forum, 2009). Unfortunately, much of the current pedagogy is based on teaching methodologies from the last century, and educational systems will need to be reinvigorated to embrace and deeply embed entrepreneurship in the way institutions operate and teach in order to meet the future needs (World Economic Forum, 2009). The World Economic Forum (2016b) affirms that building a workforce with futureproof skills will require a fundamental shift in educational models. And, while entrepreneurship champions are critical to drive change, it will also require a strong commitment from entrepreneurial leaders to be successful, as entrepreneurship is not a "nice to have," or even optional—it is a necessity in today's rapidly changing world (World Economic Forum, 2009, p. 26). Further, considering the rate of change in the Fourth Industrial Revolution, educational systems will need to respond even more rapidly than previous industrial revolutions, which took decades to respond to the demands of the labor market (World Economic Forum, 2016b).

The World Economic Forum (2009) has stated: "Entrepreneurship education is essential for developing the human capital necessary for the society of the future. It is not enough to add entrepreneurship on the perimeter—it needs to be core to the way education operates" (p. 9). The new educational model must move entrepreneurship from the perimeter to the core in order to produce the entrepreneurial workforce needed to overcome the challenges faced by the Fourth Industrial Revolution and the future of work.

Shifting Entrepreneurship From the Perimeter to the Core of Education

More often than not, entrepreneurship is not widely embraced in academia, and, while it tends to struggle to find a home in institutions, it often lands in the business school as a course or program of study (World Economic Forum, 2009). This is a result of preconceived notions of what entrepreneurship is and the connotations (often negative) around it.

For some, entrepreneurship draws up images of a greedy businessperson looking to profit off the vulnerable. For others, an image of a small business owner on Main Street comes to mind. Often, entrepreneurs are viewed as unfathomable mystery people who must have been born with special DNA or who have won the entrepreneurial lottery; they have an advantage that others simply do not have. This perception may stem from media focus on individuals such as Bill Gates, Richard Branson, and Mark Zuckerberg, often overlooking their own humble, improvised origins.

In academia, entrepreneurship can be viewed as an academic discipline in the business college for a small minority of self-selecting students who want to start a business. The curriculum tends to either focus on plan and pitch approaches with the ultimate goal of seeking venture funding or a small business management program teaching business planning, marketing, sales, accounting, and legal skills. Alarmingly, there is a disconnect between how *entrepreneurship* is traditionally defined and the actual practice of it. Therefore, we must first redefine entrepreneurship in a way that anyone can embrace it.

Redefining Entrepreneurship

George Land's (1992) transformation theory in the seminal book *Breakpoint and Beyond* can aid our understanding of entrepreneurship significantly. There are three distinct phases of transformation with various breakpoints where the rules for success change. He emphasizes that while the rules of transformation stem from the rules of nature itself, they equally apply to individuals, relationships, classrooms, organizations, society, or any type of system. For this explanation, we'll apply transformation theory to idea evolution where one is seeking to solve a problem for other people. The following is an overview of the three phases of transformation.

The Search Phase

In the search phase, the environment is highly ambiguous, and there are limited resources to solve the problem. It is an unpredictable, exploratory phase of experimentation and trial and error that is often met with frustration or great triumph. This phase consists of seeking connections in which the idea can add value to its environment. Sometimes connections are never made, and the first breakpoint never occurs (the idea dies). However, if a connection is made (a breakpoint), the connection is capitalized and the growth phase kicks in.

The Growth Phase

In the growth phase, the environment becomes less ambiguous (there are more knowns), and resources are starting to grow as value is created. The goal is to replicate the formula that previously worked and make improvements in order to grow that value. Sometimes, the replication can lead to tremendous growth very quickly, wherein resources become substantial and ambiguity is very minimal. Every system has a limitation to growth, and the success of the system itself can change the environment it lives in, thus creating new problems to solve. A comfortable, routine environment in the growth phase can lead to complacency and the complete oversight that a new phase has been reached (Land & Jarman, 1992). At this breakpoint, there is a risk of obsolescence where the idea fails to adapt to a changing environment and the resources are consumed.

The Obsolescence (Reinvention) Phase

Essentially, the last phase can lead to obsolescence if ignorance and arrogance is the chosen path, or it can be a phase of innovation where the original idea evolves and adapts based on new information and a new environment (reinvention). If the latter occurs, the third phase overlaps with the first phase as it returns to the search process. It requires new behavior and the adoption of ideas previously rejected. In fact, "Many of the things an organization said it would never do while it was in the second phase, are exactly what it will be doing in the third" (Land & Jarman, 1992, p. 68).

The transition from the second to the third phase can be much more challenging than the first to the second phase, as the organization struggles by continuing to use past successes to solve new problems (Land & Jarman, 1992). The third phase requires a major break with the past, which is challenging as the blinders of the second phase can cause an unleashing of an impenetrable defense mechanism and resistance to change. As the third phase focuses on realizing the organization's potential, it requires a revolutionary shift to reinvent itself (Land & Jarman, 1992).

The central aspects of transformation theory are the connection points (or breakpoints) between each phase and the ability to identify phases throughout an entrepreneurial journey. Each phase requires different rules and skill sets. When we distinguish the rules of survival for the search and growth phases, we redefine entrepreneurship beyond traditional notions (Figure 1.1).

The search phase is a period of experimentation during which problem-finding and problem-solving occurs. It requires inquiry, observation, adaptation, and experimentation. It requires strong communication skills and empathy in order to interact and learn from key stakeholders impacted by the problem. And to that end, it requires curiosity to continue to learn more in order to solve the problem. Collaboration is key, as teams work to make progress on finding a problem-solution fit. They are compelled

Figure 1.1. Transformation theory.

Note. Entrepreneurial Learning Initiative, n.d.; adapted from research by Land & Jarman, 1992. Reprinted with permission.

by the problem they are trying to solve, resulting in a commitment to the process and the ability to overcome self-doubt, challenges, and adversity. This, in turn, drives initiative, engagement, and self-direction in the work being done. The search phase further requires resourcefulness in a highly ambiguous, resource-constrained environment as value hasn't yet been created, and it remains uncertain whether the problem is worth solving. Finally, it requires creative and critical thinking to continue to adapt the problem-solution fit in order to make a connection. In short, many of the skills in the search phase align quite closely with the World Economic Forum's twenty-first-century skills and the demands of employers.

Traditionally, entrepreneurship has been perceived through a growth phase lens as synonymous with management, which requires delivery skills. But, *entrepreneurship is not management*. While delivery skills are very important for existing organizations, they do not accurately represent the entrepreneurial process. Entrepreneurship is a search process, and it requires discovery skills. To engage in entrepreneurship is to engage in what the Entrepreneurial Learning Initiative has termed *Opportunity Discovery*. Opportunity Discovery (Box 1.1) requires inquiry and observation, adaptation and experimentation,

BOX 1.1
Entrepreneurial Student Spotlight

The following is how Pikes Peak Community College (PPCC) student Israel Lucero applied this thinking. In the fall of 2014, Lucero enrolled at PPCC, an NACCE member college in Colorado Springs, Colorado. He was a little uncertain of his path forward. Upon enrollment, he learned that he was required to take a student success course. When he started the course, he realized that the course was being delivered using the Ice House Student Success Program, an experiential problem-based learning program. The program is designed to equip students with the perseverance and determination of an entrepreneurial mindset at the onset of their academic journey, empowering them to take ownership of their future while developing the entrepreneurial attitudes, behaviors, and skills needed to succeed in life.

Lucero quickly found himself excited for the class and the opportunity to be creative. He found himself reading ahead in the course, looking to see how he could apply the lessons. He loved the focus on finding a problem to solve in the community and how it helped connect him to positive, success-oriented people. When Lucero took an assessment on how students learn, he became curious about the alignment between how students learn and how teachers teach. In the search process, he learned that community colleges have a significant attrition problem—that students drop out of college and rarely return. He discovered that this problem could be an opportunity in that it could be a teacher–student alignment issue.

During the Opportunity Discovery Process, Israel decided to micro-experiment with the idea. He and his team built an application called Bahuka, where students could complete an assessment, explore faculty teaching philosophies, and register for classes in which the teaching philosophy aligned with how the student learned. Lucero and his team had to continue to seek new knowledge, interview stakeholders, and adapt accordingly. In a big win for the team, PPCC agreed to beta the application.

In reflection, Lucero shared how he was hyperengaged in solving the problem and that working on the project was a thrill. He was always looking for ways to do it better. He realized that he needed his academics to help him move his idea forward. Initially, he had considered his marketing class just a degree requirement, but he soon learned what he needed to know to propel his ideas further. With a broader perspective, Israel shared how an entrepreneurial mindset could contribute to human progress if it were adopted more widely.

(Continues)

Box 1.1 (*Continued*)

> With an entrepreneurial mindset, Lucero ultimately received his Associate of Arts in accounting at PPCC, while working for the college as a data entry clerk and then advancing to a junior web developer. He is now a student at the University of Colorado Colorado Springs studying for his bachelor's degree in accounting.

creative and critical thinking, communication and teamwork, perseverance and determination. What it does not require is an Ivy League degree, venture capital, a successful business plan, a unique personality or DNA, a big idea, or even an interest in business (Taulbert & Schoeniger, 2010). This perspective opens entrepreneurship up to anyone as anyone can search, and anyone can develop discovery skills.

The key is understanding that it is our responsibility to be useful to our fellow human beings. As such, we must align our interests, skills, and abilities with the needs of others to solve problems that we care about. As Google's chief education evangelist, Jaime Casap insists: "Let's stop asking kids what they want to be when they grow up. Ask them what problems they want to solve and what they need to learn in order to solve those problems" (Casap, 2014). Problem-solving drives entrepreneurial behavior and education, as it pushes students to learn how they can solve problems.

In order to truly engage students, they must take ownership of their learning. In order for them to take ownership, they have to care about the problem they are trying to solve. When we approach learning with an experiential, problem-based learning approach, engaging students in the search process to cultivate discovery skills, they become more self-directed. When students are self-directed, ownership takes place. We move students from dependent learners, in need of an authority figure with expertise to share knowledge and provide instruction, to independent learners who set their own goals and seek their own knowledge sources to achieve their goals. This is the difference between a graduate who shows up to the workforce requiring direction versus the solution-oriented, self-directed graduate who takes initiative to find problems to solve. By shifting entrepreneurial learning to the core of education, we engage students in the search process and produce entrepreneurial graduates with twenty-first-century skills needed to succeed in the new world of work.

It is not insignificant that entrepreneurial learning can lead to student engagement in education. According to Gallup, student engagement drops by 32% from elementary to high school in what is called "the school cliff" (Busteed, 2013). Colleges face similar engagement challenges, which prevent students from persisting to goal completion (Box 1.2). In addition to increasing student engagement, entrepreneurship education has been linked to higher academic achievement (Osborne, 2015). In a New York University study of students who engaged in entrepreneurial mindset curriculum, 90% of the students indicated that an entrepreneurial mindset empowered them to be successful in other academic areas, including math, writing, and research, and 95% viewed the entrepreneurial mindset as a life skill (Network for Teaching Entrepreneurship, 2015).

The search process can engage students and workers in solving problems they care about, turning problems into opportunities. While search helps us understand the entrepreneurial process, we must also examine the entrepreneurial person and the mindset that allows entrepreneurs to see opportunity while others see none.

BOX 1.2
Entrepreneurial College Spotlight

One entrepreneurial college, Edmonds Community College (EDCC), saw an increase in long-term academic achievement. EDCC, a public community college in the metropolitan area of Seattle, Washington, enrolls approximately 11,000 students a year. With a focus on innovation, inclusion, and a global perspective, EDCC is committed to academic excellence, student success, and community engagement.

In 2013, select EDCC faculty became certified to facilitate the Entrepreneurial Learning Initiative's Ice House Entrepreneurship Program. EDCC then delivered the program in one of their highest enrollment, lowest completion courses with an at-risk student population.

In conducting a comparative data study between the traditional curriculum and the Ice House curriculum, they learned that 100% of the Ice House students completed the course (no course attrition), and 90% returned the following semester. Significantly, EDCC followed the students over a 3-year period and saw an increase in academic achievement overall with 74% of Ice House students receiving GPAs in the 3.0 to 4.0 range, which was 32% more than the non-Ice House students.

Overall, EDCC's focus on implementing entrepreneurial mindset curriculum to reduce student attrition, increase student persistence, and impact overall academic achievement was very successful. In 2017, EDCC expanded its efforts with an "Entrepreneurship Across the Curriculum" initiative in which 25 additional faculty and staff were trained as Certified Ice House Facilitators to bring Ice House curriculum to EDCC in a broader, more comprehensive, interdisciplinary way.

Inside the Entrepreneurial Mindset

At this point, it's clear that entrepreneurship is much more than an academic discipline, business creation, or small business management. Entrepreneurship is a mindset, a framework for thinking and acting that can empower anyone to succeed (Taulbert & Schoeniger, 2010). It is important to understand the key constructs behind the entrepreneurial mindset, the underlying beliefs, assumptions, and thought processes that drive the behavior in order to know how to cultivate it.

The entrepreneurial person's underlying beliefs and assumptions allow them to see opportunity when others see none. At the core of that mindset is the belief that it is our responsibility to leverage our interests, skills, and abilities to be useful to others. Through such, we create value and we empower ourselves. The five key constructs supporting that core belief are self-efficacy, internal locus of control, growth mindset, intrinsic motivation, and resiliency (Figure 1.2).

By defining each construct, we see the correlation and overlap between each. Self-efficacy is the belief that individuals can achieve their goals

Figure 1.2. The five key constructs.

CORE BELIEF
It is my responsibility to figure out how to leverage my
interests, skills, and abilities to become useful to others.

Note. The Entrepreneurial Learning Initiative, n.d. Reprinted with permission.

(Bandura, 1994), which impacts their ability to cope and persist when faced with obstacles. An internal locus of control is the belief that the individual is responsible and has control over the outcomes of his or her life, as opposed to an external locus of control where the belief is that external forces (e.g., luck, fate, circumstance) influence life outcomes. Those with an internal locus of control attribute success to their own hard work as opposed to luck (Rotter, 1966). A growth mindset is the belief that skills can be developed through deliberate practice, whereas a fixed mindset is the belief that one has fixed traits of intelligence and abilities. Those with a growth mindset focus on learning goals as opposed to performance goals (e.g., grades, positive evaluations, etc.) (Dweck, 2006). Intrinsic motivation is where the performance of an activity itself naturally satisfies one (e.g., reading for the sake of reading), rather than performing the activity for an external reward (e.g., money, grade, prize, etc.) (Deci, Vallerand, Pelletier, & Ryan, 1991). And finally, resiliency is the ability to successfully adapt to adverse events by optimistically interpreting them as temporary, local, and fixable as opposed to a pessimistic interpretation that challenges are permanent, global, and unfixable (Seligman, 1990).

While each has a sliding scale depending on the nature of the situation, entrepreneurial people tend to exhibit higher levels of self-efficacy, internal locus of control, and growth mindset, which allows them to optimistically interpret and even leverage adverse situations. And, contrary to popular belief about entrepreneurial people, they tend to be intrinsically motivated —compelled by the problem they are trying to solve as opposed to extrinsic rewards. While all of these constructs can be developed, the entrepreneurial mindset is often implicitly acquired without awareness, which is often why it appears on the surface as being hereditary or a personality trait. In fact, humans are born with a natural instinct to connect with their environment and be entrepreneurial (Land & Jarman, 1992). Nonentrepreneurial behavior is often learned in systems of learning that dampen the natural instinct of children to be entrepreneurial when presented with only one way to think and act (Schramm, 2006). As the inventor, Buckminster Fuller, stated: "Everyone is born a genius. Society de-geniuses them" (Land & Jarman, 1992, p. 35).

Yet, what can be learned can be unlearned, and then learned again differently. We must remember that "the great advances in life rarely come about as the result of doing more of what we are already doing. They come about as the result of a shift in our awareness followed by a change in our behavior" (Taulbert & Schoeniger, 2010, p. 176). An entrepreneurial mindset can be learned, but we must create entrepreneurial learning environments in our classrooms and institutions to do so.

Creating Entrepreneurial Learning Environments

To develop the entrepreneurial mindset, we must look at the person, the process, and the situation. We've examined the entrepreneurial person by defining the entrepreneurial mindset and the key constructs behind it. We've examined the entrepreneurial process by redefining *entrepreneurship* as search or an Opportunity Discovery Process. We'll now examine how the situation can either encourage or discourage entrepreneurial learning environments and the development of entrepreneurial attitudes, behaviors, and skills.

In the World Economic Forum's (2009) *Educating the Next Wave of Entrepreneurs*, the Global Education Initiative, made up of the leadership of Microsoft, Cisco, Intel, Goldman Sachs, and AMD, comments, "We believe entrepreneurial skills, attitudes, and behaviors can be learned, and that exposure to entrepreneurship education throughout an individual's life-long learning path . . . is imperative" (p. 6). The report addressed entrepreneurship education in the broadest and most comprehensive manner at that time. The report goes on to state, "Not everyone needs to become an entrepreneur to benefit from entrepreneurship education, but all members of society need to be more entrepreneurial. . . . We need to create the types of environments that are conducive to encouraging entrepreneurial ways of thinking and behaving" (p. 7).

The report strongly emphasizes the need for entrepreneurship to be deeply embedded across college campuses and disciplines in order for all students and faculty to be exposed to entrepreneurship education, no matter their chosen path. To do so, the entrepreneurial mindset must be cultivated at the individual level focusing on the development of entrepreneurial attitudes, behaviors, and skills. This cultivation requires experiential learning and real engagement in the entrepreneurial process. It requires interaction with real world entrepreneurs, preferably local, to serve as socially relatable role models, a component of self-efficacy. And, it requires an entrepreneurial educator who acts as a facilitator guiding the entrepreneurial learning process so that the students take ownership of the process.

The World Economic Forum (2009) details effective aspects of an entrepreneurship program, which should

> focus on building self-confidence and self-efficacy as well as developing the practical skills necessary for students to initiate and pursue ideas, and provide them with experience in building the necessary teams around them to implement projects. Entrepreneurship education should not be limited to a focus on start-ups . . . but should be focused on shifting mindsets and developing skills which can be applied in many forms and entrepreneurial settings. (p. 20)

The World Economic Forum offers several ways for institutions to inspire and strengthen entrepreneurial learning environments, including the following:

1. Encouraging all faculty of all disciplines to expose students to entrepreneurship at every level in a cross-disciplinary environment
2. Implementing entrepreneurship education with an experiential learning model that also incorporates video case studies of real-world entrepreneurs as well as local entrepreneurs
3. Building a pipeline of entrepreneurial educators through entrepreneurial training and education (Adapted from the World Economic Forum, 2009)

Unfortunately, and perhaps even unintentionally, institutions often discourage entrepreneurial learning environments with policies, procedures, and practices that prevent entrepreneurial behavior (World Economic Forum, 2009). Entrepreneurial champions often find themselves roadblocked trying to navigate an impossible, nonentrepreneurial system. To become an entrepreneurial institution, entrepreneurship must be a part of the organizational DNA, embedded in the institution's vision, mission, and value system. Leadership must commit to leading with an entrepreneurial mindset and embracing entrepreneurship from a high level in order to achieve success.

Leading With an Entrepreneurial Mindset

Community colleges are the economic engines of their communities, producing the future workforce and often developing the existing workforce. They are in a unique position to comprehensively lead entrepreneurial efforts from the inside out. By implementing entrepreneurship curriculum in a cross-disciplinary fashion inclusive of the local entrepreneurial community, colleges build a significant bridge from the classroom to the community. Students learn from entrepreneurial people who came from similar, and sometimes worse, circumstances and were able to succeed by cultivating and employing an entrepreneurial mindset. Often, this entrepreneurial community will demystify the entrepreneurial process while becoming a network or support system for students to launch their own ideas beyond the search phase. Planting the seed of entrepreneurial thinking often spurs those who never saw themselves as entrepreneurs, those who would never have selfselected into an entrepreneurship program, to in fact, become entrepreneurs (Box 1.3).

BOX 1.3
Entrepreneurial Community Spotlight

Community is truly the new currency, and one community, the city of Albuquerque, New Mexico, understands the implications and rewards of building an entrepreneurial community to realize its potential. With the leadership of Mayor Richard Berry and NACCE member college Central New Mexico Community College (CNM) President Katharine Winograd, the city of Albuquerque took the unprecedented approach of instilling an entrepreneurial mindset in city government employees. In 2015, the city partnered with CNM as a workforce development initiative to implement the Ice House Entrepreneurship Program in an initial pilot of 100 city employees from diverse departments and positions. The goal was to empower city employees to take ownership of their work and to inspire them to apply new and innovative thinking to their jobs, thereby better serving the citizens of their community.

The program empowered employees to see problems as opportunities and to view themselves as active contributors in the organization's mission. Employees from front-line sanitation workers to high-level leaders worked in small teams to solve problems, learning how everyday entrepreneurs identify and solve problems in real world, resource-constrained circumstances using an iterative, experimental approach.

In the Opportunity Discovery Process, city sanitation workers were inspired to find a way to redesign trash and recycling pickups, which resulted in thousands of dollars of savings. Other participants focused on redesigning the city's defensive driving program to an online format, which saved taxpayers around $70,000 a year. More importantly, the city has increased the engagement level of city employees by empowering them to take ownership of their work with an entrepreneurial mindset.

The city expanded its efforts by partnering with the Albuquerque Public School District to provide a multi-district offering of Ice House to high school students. In addition, the city developed a Public Service University, training the staff as Ice House certified facilitators to deliver Ice House as part of employee orientation, management training, and department training to city employees. To date, over 500 city employees have completed Ice House, and the city has committed to implementing the program with every city employee.

"We are not just teaching people how to think like entrepreneurs, but how to view their current situation as an opportunity where innovation and creativity are encouraged. . . . Our employees are feeling empowered, they are finding their voice and returning to their jobs with a renewed

(Continues)

Box 1.3 (*Continued*)

sense of ownership, purpose, and pride," said Tom Darling, division manager of Albuquerque's Public Service University.

To learn more, visit the Unleashing Human Potential: The Key to Our City's Future website at www.mindsetmemo.com and download an e-book of their outcomes at www.elimindset.com.

Being the leader in producing an entrepreneurial workforce will reap other significant economic benefits as entrepreneurial workers tend to contribute to a culture of innovation, which will not only retain talent but also become a magnet for talent. In the new world of work, independent contractors and employees in flexible work environments get to "placemake," choosing where they want to live and work. This is a new economic development strategy that most communities have not yet strategically developed.

Takeaways

It is critical and ever-pressing that education heeds the call to move entrepreneurship from the perimeter to the core of the way it operates in order to remain relevant and avoid obsolescence. Here's how:

- Good ideas are not always new ideas. Look to improve existing ideas.
- Ideas rarely arrive fully formed. Continue to engage in the search process.
- Don't go it alone. Engage your community as it takes a village.
- Good ideas can be slow ideas, but you must go to know (as opposed to know to go).
- A failure to take some sort of action will have significant economic implications resulting in unemployment, inequality, and in turn, a diminishing consumer base for business (World Economic Forum, 2016b).
- As U.S. Army General Eric Shinseki once said, "If you don't like change, you'll like irrelevance even less." Complacency is simply not an option when it comes to education and entrepreneurship.
- *Entrepreneurship must be offered broadly and to every student.* It is not enough to offer entrepreneurship education in the business school alone, and it must not be offered solely to college students.

- Academic leaders, staff, and faculty should all engage in entrepreneurial mindset training to cultivate entrepreneurial thought and process into their work.
- Institutions must become more entrepreneurial in the way they operate, embedding it in the culture and adopting it into the value system.
- Avoid planning paralysis; experimentation is the key to discovery. To take action now, it is critical to begin by
  - fully embracing the entrepreneurial mindset;
  - consistently bringing the entrepreneurial mindset into the campus conversation, engaging interdisciplinary faculty in entrepreneurial workshops and training, and piloting entrepreneurial mindset curriculum; and
  - empowering and supporting the early adopters as they will help gain the early majority and broaden the overall adoption.
- The entrepreneurial mindset is simultaneously our future and our tool kit needed to get there. It is "transformational when embraced and experienced on a daily basis," offering "a new way in which to view the world, one that reveals new opportunities, ignites ambition, and unlocks . . . *human potential* [emphasis added]" (Taulbert & Schoeniger, 2010, p. xxix).

References

Bandura, A. (1994). Self-efficacy. *Encyclopedia of Human Behavior, 4*, 71–81.

Busteed, B. (2013). *The school cliff: Student engagement drops with each school year.* Available from http://news.gallup.com/opinion/gallup/170525/school-cliff-student-engagement-drops-school-year.aspx

CareerBuilder. (2014). *Overwhelming majority of companies say soft skills are just as important as hard skills, according to a new CareerBuilder survey.* Available from http://www.careerbuilder.com/share/aboutus/pressreleasesdetail.aspx?ed=12/31/2014&id=pr817&sd=4/10/2014

Casap, J. (2014, July 26). *Summer Leadership Institute.* Flagstaff, AZ: Arizona School Boards Association. Available from https://katielmartin.com/2017/02/05/why-we-should-stop-asking-kids-what-they-want-to-be-when-they-grow-up/

Deci, E., Vallerand, R., Pelletier, L. G., & Ryan, R. (1991). Motivation and education: The self-determination perspective. *Educational Psychologist, 26*(3 & 4), 325–346.

Dweck, C. (2006). *Mindset: The new psychology of success.* New York, NY: Random House.

Emergent Research & Intuit Inc. (2010). *Intuit 2020 report: Twenty trends that will shape the next decade.* Available from https://http-download.intuit.com/http.intuit/CMO/intuit/futureofsmallbusiness/intuit_2020_report.pdf

Entrepreneurial Learning Initiative. (n.d.). What is mindset? Available from https://
elimindset.com/entrepreneurial-learning/what-is-mindset/

Gillespie, P. (2017). *Intuit: Gig economy is 34% of US workforce.* Available from http://
money.cnn.com/2017/05/24/news/economy/gig-economy-intuit/index.html

Land, G., & Jarman, B. (1992). *Breakpoint and beyond: Mastering the future today.*
New York, NY: HarperBusiness.

Network for Teaching Entrepreneurship. (2015). *NYU study: 90% of students connect
entrepreneurial mindset to academic success.* Available from https://www.prnewswire
.com/news-releases/nyu-study-90-of-students-connect-entrepreneurial-mindset
-to-academic-success-300042079.html

Osborne, S. (2015). Life's work. *Harvard Business Review, 93*(4). Available from
https://hbr.org/2015/04/young-people-need-to-know-entrepreneurship-is-hard

Rotter, J. B. (1966). Generalized expectancies for internal versus external control of
reinforcement. *Psychological Monographs: General and Applied, (80)*1, 1–28.

Schramm, C. J. (2006). *The entrepreneurial imperative: How America's economic mir-
acle will reshape the world (and change your life).* New York, NY: Harper Collins.

Schwab, K. (2016, January 14). *The Fourth Industrial Revolution: What it means,
how to respond.* Available from https://www.weforum.org/agenda/2016/01/the-
fourth-industrial-revolution-what-it-means-and-how-to-respond

Seligman, M. E. P. (1990). *Learned optimism: How to change your mind and your life.*
New York, NY: Vintage Books.

Taulbert, C. L., & Schoeniger, G. (2010). *Who owns the ice house? Eight life lessons
from an unlikely entrepreneur.* Cleveland, OH: ELI Press.

World Economic Forum. (2009). *Executive summary: Educating the next wave of
entrepreneurs.* Geneva, SUI: World Economic Forum.

World Economic Forum. (2016a). *Executive summary: The future of jobs employment,
skills and workforce strategy for the Fourth Industrial Revolution.* Geneva, SUI:
World Economic Forum.

World Economic Forum. (2016b). *New vision for education: Fostering social and emotional learning through technology.* Geneva, SUI: World Economic Forum.

World Economic Forum. (2017). *The global human capital report 2017.* Geneva,
SUI: World Economic Forum.

World Economic Forum, & BVL International. (2017). *Impact of the Fourth Industrial Revolution on supply chains.* Geneva, SUI: World Economic Forum.

2

AN ENTREPRENEURIAL APPROACH TO ENTREPRENEURIAL EDUCATION

Andrew Gold and Mary Beth Kerly

This chapter will take the reader on a journey through the steps needed to build a meaningful, relevant, and sustainable entrepreneurship program at a community college. Readers will learn how to approach program development through the lens of a business start-up, and how the lean start-up modeling process can be applied to develop an entrepreneurship program and curriculum; how to create a canvas for developing your program; and the various teaching methodologies being used today. This chapter draws from experiences at Hillsborough Community College (HCC) as case studies for understanding many challenges facing educators, administrators, and the students at community colleges that yearn for a more robust and impactful entrepreneurship curriculum.

Building a business in a resource-constrained, uncertain economic environment is what early-stage business enterprising is largely about. Developing and launching an entrepreneurship program within a community college is no different. Overcoming factors such as trying to innovate in an innovation-resistant bureaucracy requires a combination of persistence, adaptability, creativity, and a willingness to act.

Most of all, developing an entrepreneurial program at a community college requires an entrepreneurial mindset. An entrepreneurial mindset alerts you to the fact that an inability to build something (i.e., a business, product, entrepreneurship program, etc.) is never about a lack of resources, but rather a lack of resourcefulness. In fact, scarcity of resources is the primary fuel for innovation. In the absence of resources, people are forced to innovate.

Entrepreneurship Education's Evolution

Although the concept of entrepreneurship is nothing new, the notion of delivering a curriculum related to entrepreneurship is still in its infancy. Some scholars trace entrepreneurship education back to Harvard University when a course called "New Enterprises" was offered for the first time in 1947 for returning veterans (Kauffman Foundation, 2013). Entrepreneurship education has been one of the most prominent success stories in higher education over the last few decades. While the concept of being able to teach people to become entrepreneurs was largely unknown in the 1970s, many universities began to include some entrepreneurial components especially in their business curricula in the 1980s (Kuckertz, 2013).

This trend, originally emanating from the United States, has continued throughout the 1990s and the first decade of the twenty-first century. Entrepreneurship education has grown steadily, and at a more accelerated pace over the past 10 years. According to a recent report published by the Kauffman Foundation, in partnership with Babson College, nearly 200,000 students in 2,000 colleges in the United States are currently enrolled in entrepreneurship and small business management courses.

Can Entrepreneurship Be Taught?

As the growth of entrepreneurship education has expanded, researchers have debated whether or not entrepreneurship can be taught. Many have posited that the only way a person can learn to be an entrepreneur is by being an entrepreneur. However, a preponderance of the literature revealed that entrepreneurship, or certain facets of it, *can* be taught (Kuratko, 2005).

In the book, *Born, Not Made; The Entrepreneurial Personality* (Fisher & Koch, 2008), James Koch suggests that some people may be born with an entrepreneurial gene. However, what if that entrepreneurial gene becomes dormant, or at a minimum stigmatized by society, as an imaginative, creative, and entrepreneurial child grows up and learns to stop dreaming and starts focusing on a core academic pursuit? If the gene is indeed dormant, perhaps the entrepreneurial desire simply needs to be reignited through entrepreneurship education. Still, many reject the notion of an entrepreneurial gene. Peter Drucker (1985), one of the leading management thinkers of our time, recognized that: "The entrepreneurial mystique? It is not magic, it is not mysterious, and it has nothing to do with the genes. It's a discipline, and like any discipline, it can be learned" (p. 121). Most entrepreneurship educators would concur with Drucker, and in fact have seen that entrepreneurship can indeed be taught in some form.

However, being able to teach someone about something, doesn't mean they will become proficient in the practice of what they have been taught. For example, we know that science can be taught, but this does not mean that a student of science will be able to effectively practice science. The same is true of entrepreneurship. Learning about entrepreneurship does not qualify a person to practice entrepreneurship; it simply allows a person to increase their entrepreneurial literacy.

Whether you think entrepreneurship can be taught, or whether people are born entrepreneurs and simply need to reconnect with their entrepreneurial spirit, a more important question is: What is the best way to teach entrepreneurship (Ronstadt, 1987)?

Does Culture Matter?

Institutional culture is critical to developing an entrepreneurship program. Laura Palmer-Noone (2000) summarized the core problem facing many institutions of higher learning when she wrote, "Inertia is a villain in the marketplace but is worshiped in higher education because we relish tradition" (p. 3). Leaders of businesses know what stagnation can do to a business. Scott Cook, cofounder of Intuit (Quicken, QuickBooks, and TurboTax), is an advocate of the new lean start-up educational paradigm. Cook reflected on the thin line between success and failure when he said, "Success is a powerful thing. It tends to make companies stupid, and they become less and less innovative" (Nobel, 2013). According to Cook, avoiding innovation stagnation is what separates a successful leader from an average one. Cook believes not only that the lean start-up method serves start-up businesses well but also established companies need a lean start-up model (Nobel, 2013).

Many colleges claim they promote innovation, but their culture says otherwise. The slow-moving nature of many college cultures can work well with certain disciplines, but entrepreneurship is not one of them. Institutions that wish to develop robust and dynamic entrepreneurial programs need to overcome internal inertia (Palmer-Noone, 2000).

The primary outcome for entrepreneurship programs developed in non-innovative colleges is that new programs are bogged down in a status quo of slow, stop, and wait. In these institutions, because there is such a lag time to launch, by the time the program interacts with students, it is already obsolete. Another potential outcome from cultures that promote slow, stop, and wait is that program developers become worn down and cease to develop (Palmer-Noone, 2000). Both outcomes are not in the best interests of students, and while many administrators appear to recognize this dichotomy, little is being done to fix it (Palmer-Noone, 2000).

Consequently, many colleges have been slow to adopt the newer, more innovative forms of entrepreneurial education because they require rapid decision-making, centralized control, and constant modification and development—all conflicting with the inherent culture of inertia. In addition, many faculty members may lack the requisite skills to execute the new framework for teaching entrepreneurship or the desire to learn a new method (Singh, 2008).

At the core of inertia, one will often find an organizational culture that is fearful of failure. Entrepreneurs know that a fear of failure can only accomplish one of two things: either stop you from starting, or stop you from stopping. Both are bad. On the other hand, the concept of loss aversion (Tversky & Kahneman, 1991) informs us that if you are brave enough to try and take action on something, and it does not work out, it is better to keep working on a failed project than admit that you have failed to avoid facing the perceived shame that comes along with failure.

But what if we leveraged an entrepreneurial mindset across the community college domain and redefined the meaning of failure? This would involve an organizational culture that applauded those that failed as loudly as we applaud success. Imagine the transformational change that might occur within that college! Faculty, staff, and administrators would feel empowered to give things a go, to try and add value through innovative practices, knowing that whether the initiative was a success or a failure, accolades would be delivered. This would, in turn, lower the level of employee disengagement and better serve students, while also informing universities of potential new programs that could be deployed. Transformational change in the education system and workplace needs to occur, so that people think of and define *failure* in a more constructive light. Astro Teller (2016) from Google X, says:

> We work hard at X to make it safe to fail. Teams kill their ideas as soon as the evidence is on the table because they're rewarded for it. They get applause from their peers. Hugs and high fives from their manager, me in particular. They get promoted for it. We have bonused every single person on teams that ended their projects, from teams as small as two to teams of more than 30. We believe in dreams at the moonshot factory. But enthusiastic skepticism is not the enemy of boundless optimism. It's optimism's perfect partner. It unlocks the potential in every idea.

Failure can be redefined as the moment when you realize what you are working on does not, and will not work, and yet you continue to work on that thing. All the steps that led up to that moment when you realize that what you have been working on is flawed can simply be viewed as valuable learning. Colleges that integrate an entrepreneurial mindset across the entire organization are realizing the rewards that come along with thinking as an entrepreneurial organization.

Entrepreneurship is a way of thinking or embracing certain conventions that promote action. These actions are designed to promote learning and solution searching, coupled with innovations that can add value. This action-oriented mindset is accompanied by a series of intangible skills such as having an internal locus of control, a growth mindset, strong sense of self-efficacy, perseverance, adaptability, an ability to think big, creativity, resourcefulness, and an ability to understand and cope with failure in a different light. Colleges that embrace an entrepreneurial culture are positioned to lead in education innovation.

Moving From the Plan and Pitch Teaching Method to Show and Tell

For some colleges that have been teaching entrepreneurship for a while, business planning has been the cornerstone of most entrepreneurship courses and curriculum. There is good reason for this; practice helped inform the education field, and the message was clear. As Steve Blank (2013) stated in his *Harvard Business Review* article titled, "Why the Lean Start-Up Changes Everything," "According to conventional wisdom, the first thing every founder must do is create a business plan—a static document that describes the size of an opportunity, the problem to be solved, and the solution that the new venture will provide." Business plans usually include a five-year financial forecast as well. According to Blank, this approach is flawed for many reasons. The business plan is largely built on unproven assumptions. Perhaps even more problematic is that a business plan assumes that a start-up business idea is a smaller version of a large corporation. Because of this, the business plan places undue attention on presenting unproven assumptions as facts and telling the reader why a business idea is compelling, rather than showing the reader, through validated proof, that the idea is actually viable.

There is a time for business planning, but that time comes after a business has started and is able to demonstrate that it has reached the stage of executing a repeatable and functional business model. The culture of some higher education institutions remains tethered to the older status quo methods of teaching entrepreneurship through business planning. Academics continue to debate whether traditional entrepreneurship can or should still be taught, especially considering the cultural barriers to developing the pedagogy. However, while this debate goes on, practical entrepreneurs have made transformational changes within their field to develop new methods for starting businesses with far less risk. These strategies are eminently teachable. The lean start-up, business model generation movement began about 10 years ago, and its success has been substantial (Blank, 2013). Scott Benjamin, director of the Center of Entrepreneurship at Florida Institute of Technology, cites the benefits of the lean start-up model:

> While I teach business plan research, I'm quickly becoming a believer in the lean launchpad. Traditional start-up methods encourage students to sit at their computers and gather industry reports and census data, whereas lean methods require students to engage customers in a dialogue about product development. Though I see merit in both approaches, I'd rather have my students trained in interacting with prospects than crunching another mythical financial statement. (S. Benjamin, personal communication, August 20, 2018)

The core of the lean start-up methodology involves rapid hypothesis testing of various business model assumptions that comprise a business model. By engaging potential customers, suppliers, and other stakeholders, and then either pivoting to another iteration of the idea or persevering by launching a business around tested and valid findings, the entrepreneur has gained valuable insights. This highly experiential model for entrepreneurial education is disruptive to typical college cultures, which are typically slow at enacting program changes because of deeply institutionalized processes that inhibit innovation and exploration.

New Economic Problems Create Opportunities

The timing of this new method for delivering entrepreneurial education comes at a very good time. The changing landscape of our economy demands that students involve themselves in entrepreneurial education. For decades, it was common for students to enter the workforce (career escalator) after getting a high school or college degree. Once on this career escalator, people would slowly rise, gaining wage increases, benefits, and pensions. Eventually, people would elect to step off the escalator, retire, and enjoy the rest of their lives. Today, this paradigm appears to be broken. Workers are simply not getting off the escalator. *Why?* Perhaps because they like their job, maybe they did not save adequately, or perhaps it is because people are living longer. No matter what the reason might be, this new era is causing congestion all the way down to the bottom of the escalator, where it is becoming increasingly difficult for students to step on. In addition, other people are being involuntarily thrown off the escalator because their skills are no longer in demand.

On the surface, many argue that this problem is serious and poses a severe threat to our long-term economic outlook. However, this new economic reality is in fact a great opportunity, specifically for the innovative culture of community colleges because a relevant entrepreneurship curriculum provides a solution to this problem. People now have the chance, with innovative experiential teaching methods, to begin investing in themselves and learning entrepreneurial skills, such as creativity, thinking innovatively, finding and solving problems, effectively managing risk, adaptability, and so on. Whether you desire to start your own business or work for an existing company, all of these soft skills are the high demand skills needed today (Bauer-Wolf, 2018).

Traditional employers do not want to invest in training; rather, employers look to employees to bring innovative ways of thinking that add immediate value to the enterprise. No longer is it sufficient to work purely as an accountant or engineer. Today's global marketplace demands that these specialists add value by effectively managing risk, identifying meaningful problems, and cocreating efficient solutions in an innovative and adaptable fashion, all attributes of entrepreneurs.

To help launch its entrepreneurship program, HCC designed a new tool called the Community Engagement and E-ship Education Canvas (Table 2.1). This Canvas, like the business model and lean canvas, provides community college faculty champions with an opportunity to apply the hypothesis testing, scientific method used in the lean start-up methodology to program development within a community college.

The flow of the Canvas begins in the upper left-hand corner with the Purpose, followed by Measure and Jump the Walls. These elements are done in order. Engagement occurs during these three phases—as it is required for each element. Serving as the foundation for the top of the Canvas is Champions and Money Matters; without these elements the Canvas begins to fall apart. The most critical part of the Canvas is Embracing Failure and developing a culture within the institution that supports risk-taking and makes the Champions feel safe from failure.

Following is a case study on the Canvas model.

Purpose

At the onset of the development of building the entrepreneurship program, we assessed the current situation using effectual reasoning. There was not a specific goal in mind, such as offering a new course or degree, or even one to increase student enrollment. Rather, we started with what we knew: Interest in entrepreneurship was increasing within our state. An article in *Fast Company* magazine in May of 2013 titled, "A Sunny Outcome: Why Florida Startups Are Soaring High" (www.fit.edu/faculty-profiles/7/scott-benjamin/?tracks=sbenjamin), mentioned Tampa Bay as being a highly collaborative city when it comes to building an entrepreneurial ecosystem. Additionally, television shows like *Shark Tank* and *The Profit* were gaining popularity, which was an anecdotal indicator that entrepreneurship would be of interest to our students. Previously, television shows such as *Hell's Kitchen*, *Cake Boss*, and *Top Chef* led to increased interest among students in culinary programs, just as *CSI* and *Law and Order* increased interest in police, criminal justice, and crime-scene curriculum.

TABLE 2.1
Community Engagement and E-Ship Education Canvas

Purpose	Measure	Jump the Walls
• Identify need/opportunity • Find a niche • Identify your program purpose—your "why?" • Use design thinking to establish empathy with students, faculty, staff, and community partners	• Avoid "build it and they will come" mentality • Collect data, validate ad hoc, internal primary research, community input	• Get out of home institution • Conferences, cold calls, networking organizations • Visit and speak with other colleges • Identify subject matter experts, develop entrepreneur in residence, engage local entrepreneurs, create internships
Engage Build momentum by creating new events, modify existing curriculum, design new programs/courses, organize internships, leverage advisory board, recruit students		
Champion(s) Two if possible: faculty, staff, or administrator committed to the effort	**Money Matters** Grants, fund-raising, institutional activity funds, student fees	
Embrace Failure Develop a culture that rewards risk-taking with a structure that supports innovation		

Measurement

Although we had anecdotal evidence that there was an interest in entrepreneurship, we knew that we had to determine if there was a demand for an academic program. We had tried the "build it and they will come" approach in 2009 with the introduction of the Business Development and Entrepreneurship 25 College Credit Certificate (CCC). While it served as a pathway to an associate's degree in business administration, there were very few completers (three completers between 2009 and 2013), an unknown track record regarding students opening their own businesses, and on close inspection, the certificate was an entrepreneurship certificate in name only, as the courses required for completion were standard business administration course offerings. By all accounts, the certificate was a failure, and we were determined to learn from that experience about what not to do moving forward.

In the fall of 2013, prior to the development of any additional academic programs, a survey about various dimensions of entrepreneurship education and interest levels in entrepreneurship was developed in partnership with the institutional research department. This survey went to all 45,000 HCC students and generated a sample of respondents ($n = 1,555$). The findings indicated that students wanted a 12-CCC in entrepreneurship that could be completed in a single semester. In addition, the data showed that an overwhelming number of students wanted to take the courses in-class ($n = 1,188$), and they wanted to track through the program in a cohort. Our research further indicated which topics within a potential entrepreneurship program would be most beneficial to students (finance, managing a business, sales and marketing, and cocurricular activities).

Jump the Walls

The effectual thinking principle of "bird-in-the-hand," suggests reflecting on *who* you know as well as *what* you know. So, having understood the problem and measuring interest, it was time to jump the walls of HCC and begin to interact with our community to validate our assumptions and quantitative research. One of the entrepreneurship team members was new to Tampa Bay and did not know anyone in the community. He leveraged LinkedIn, stumbled upon an entrepreneur in the Tampa Bay community who was involved in many entrepreneurial programs, set up a chance meeting, and that meeting led to countless opportunities for the HCC entrepreneurship team. Years later, it led to a gift in perpetuity to the HCC entrepreneurship program.

This story is an example of the effectuation lemonade principle, which espouses embracing lemons (not knowing anyone in the entrepreneurship ecosystem) and making lemonade (getting plugged into the entire ecosystem through a random interaction with a community connector), but also speaks to the power of serendipity. During the spring and summer of 2013, members of the entrepreneurship team met with more than 57 members of the Tampa Bay entrepreneurial ecosystem to seek input, direction, feedback, and help with developing programs that would help to support the new certificate program.

Beginning in 2012 the team jumped the walls of HCC and began to seek out key players in the Tampa Bay entrepreneurial ecosystem. Using social media, Greater Tampa Chamber of Commerce meet-and-greets, and good old-fashioned networking, the team began to put together a new business advisory board and lay the groundwork for excitement in the community. Each meeting generated a new contact and another scheduled meeting. This process was and continues to be relentless. It is important to note that each new contact resulted in a mutually beneficial relationship. Community contacts were not approached with what they could do for us, but rather how we could help each other and have a long-term relationship. It's worthwhile to note that one of HCC's institutional values is to anticipate and respond to community needs.

The community added value by providing thoughtful input to the academic program and the cocurricular activities that would support it. The result was the creation of a brand new 12-credit CCC in entrepreneurship and innovation that included two new courses that needed to be developed and approved by the Academic Affairs Committee, the Board of Trustees, and the Florida State Department of Education. We also garnered multiple ideas for workshops, events, and celebrations in the process.

Engagement

Engagement varies from stakeholder to stakeholder. More engagement spurs more opportunities. Building on the effectuation model, the lemonade principle maintains that when unexpected things happen, whether good or bad, opportunities arise.

Hosting a large-scale, college-wide community event provides a platform for a campus to engage with other faculty, staff, students, administrators, and members of the community. In the spring of 2013, the entrepreneurship team hosted 2 events themed around entrepreneurship on the Dale Mabry Campus. An average of 127 students attended each event. In the fall of that same year, the entrepreneurship team hosted and promoted 5 events, including an all-day Veterans Entrepreneurship Training Symposium (VETS).

To create momentum, the team identified one target market of the new entrepreneurship program and designed a one-day event specific to the needs of veterans. This population was a good fit because the college already had resources in place, including the veterans advising office and a host of secondary research indicating that veterans were engaging in entrepreneurship in greater numbers. A cross-functional team, including the HCC Foundation, marketing, student clubs, advising, deans, faculty, and community members partnered to execute the day's activities.

During the event, guest speakers (several of our new community partners), engaged participants during workshops on various entrepreneurial topics. Local CEOs served as Shark Tank "judges," and HCC students volunteered as greeters and event coordinators.

Engagement increases substantially when members of the community hear about your efforts. In coordination with HCC's marketing department, we have been able to consistently secure media placements about the HCC entrepreneurship program. The entrepreneurship team receives consistent feedback from students and community leaders that affirms there is a need for a place where people can go to find out about available entrepreneurship resources. A college-wide website serves as an ecosystem hub for resources in the Tampa Bay Entrepreneurial Ecosystem. The website is also a valuable resource for listing community events as well as local partners and donors (https://hccfl.edu/innovation).

Engagement with students is a key factor in developing these programs. One method of engaging students (with the community) is through internships. Internships are a critical component of the entrepreneurship program overall and the academic certificate specifically. They provide students with additional experiential learning opportunities, networking, and mentoring.

The HCC team secured its first internship site in the spring of 2013 at Tampa Bay Wave, a technology business incubator located in downtown Tampa. Two students who participated in this internship during the summer and fall of 2013 had exceptional experiences, and they were able to secure part-time employment resulting from their internships. Since that time, the HCC team has been able to secure additional internships and continues to grow this program.

One of the major tenets of any business is to create customers. Tuition growth (in academia), and profit growth (in the private sector) are metrics of how good you are at creating customers. One of the initial barriers to enrolling students into the certificate program was that one of the four courses in the certificate (SBM 2000) had prerequisites. In many instances, the entrepreneurship team, in an effort to recruit a cohort of students, was able to remove the prerequisites, thus making enrollment efforts into SBM 2000 much easier.

Because HCC's program is striving to become a recognized leader in entrepreneurship education, it is imperative to engage with other academic institutions, share and exchange ideas, and find common ground to collaborate. Before the academic program began, HCC's entrepreneurship team recruited graduate students at the University of Tampa, undergraduate students at the University of South Florida, and faculty at Saint Petersburg College to collaborate and exchange ideas about program development. The Tampa Bay area offers an impressive array of entrepreneurship programs. By engaging other academic institutions, we are able to gain valuable guidance and identify opportunities to network and grow the HCC program.

Money Matters

In a resource-constrained environment such as a community college, finding financial resources is challenging. College-sponsored events that create engagement provide companies with the opportunity to provide sponsorships.

Beginning in the spring and summer of 2013, the entrepreneurship team met with the leadership of the HCC Foundation to map out a fund-raising strategy for the VETS business pitch competition prize awards, scholarships, and general funds for the development of the entrepreneurship program. This partnership was unique in several ways. First, it demonstrated a model for faculty members to engage and coordinate with the HCC Foundation. Second, because the VETS event was the first of its kind at HCC, it served as an opportunity for the entrepreneurship team to introduce the foundation to new sources of funding in the Tampa Bay entrepreneurship ecosystem.

Over a 4-month period, HCC was able to raise $39,600. These funds were a critical benchmark to have in place prior to the launch of the academic program because they indicated strong community support and provided money for continued promotion of the program prior to the launch of the academic certificate program.

By "Jumping the Walls," the entrepreneurship team was able to compete for and secure a $15,000 grant from the Coleman Foundation in the fall of 2013. In partnership with the HCC Foundation, the entrepreneurship team was also able to secure a $5,000 grant from the Hillsborough County Economic Development Innovation Initiative (EDI2).

Champion

Building the academic entrepreneurship education portion of this model required a minimum of one full-time faculty member, or "champion" who was willing to engage in growing the entire program (curricular and cocurricular) through extensive faculty development, including professional memberships, conference presentations, publishing, webinars, and so on.

In August 2012, HCC hired a new full-time faculty member, Andy Gold, to join Mary Beth Kerly, who was also a full-time faculty member. Gold brought to HCC 20-plus years as an entrepreneur and extensive experience developing entrepreneurship programs. Prior to launching the academic program in January 2014, the entrepreneurship team had collectively engaged in extensive faculty development, conference presentations, and publishing.

The groundwork of this effort had begun in the fall of 2012 (and continues today) with the HCC entrepreneurship team spending countless hours traveling around the Tampa area to meet and develop new relationships with critical members of the local entrepreneurial ecosystem. This was done voluntarily; however, in retrospect it speaks to the passion and commitment of the entrepreneurship team to build a great program.

In many instances, the volunteer time (gift-in-kind) of the entrepreneurship team has been extensive. Taking ownership of the program and serving as volunteers prior to the launch of the academic program sent a strong message to our community partners that we were genuinely concerned and passionate about building the entrepreneurship program at HCC.

All of this was done without additional compensation to the champion, one of the most critical drivers in developing a successful program. The initial development of an entrepreneurship program must be driven by a full-time faculty member willing to volunteer his/her time outside of the institution to engage with the community. While a faculty champion is required for academic development, it is just as imperative to have an internal champion within the college's administration and staff.

Embrace Failure

Bureaucratic institutions, including community colleges, are not built to embrace failure. However, effectual logic tells us that failure can create opportunities. So, *how does a community college balance bureaucratic requirements with a culture of innovation?*

The entrepreneurship team held continuous meetings with the campus dean, campus president, and administrators at the district office to share progress and obtain feedback. This step is critical because in order for the program to flourish and succeed, support must be attained at the highest levels of the institution. Without buy-in from internal stakeholders, barriers begin to crop up, which slows down innovation and progress.

Where Are We Today?

The HCC entrepreneurship program has made enormous progress over the past 5 years. The Business Advisory Board has grown from 4 members to nearly 30. The current academic framework includes a 12-CCC in Entrepreneurship and Innovation, a revamped 25-CCC in Business Development and Entrepreneurship, an associate's degree in Entrepreneurship and a Transfer Track in Entrepreneurship. The program has hosted a wide array of campus events and programs to promote and create awareness for entrepreneurship, drawing over 1,000 students to these events.

HCC stands on the leading edge of how entrepreneurship is taught and how new programs can be developed. Community colleges interested in establishing vibrant entrepreneurship programs can do so by following the steps outlined in the model presented here, prudently using resources, and gaining a commitment from all levels of the administration.

Takeaways

- The slow-moving nature of many college cultures can work well with certain disciplines, but entrepreneurship is not one of them.
- Transformational change in the education system and workplace needs to occur so that people think of and define failure in a more constructive light.
- The Canvas provides community college champions with an opportunity to apply the scientific method used in the lean start-up methodology to program development within a community college.
- Engagement varies from stakeholder to stakeholder. More engagement spurs more opportunities.
- While a faculty champion is required for academic development, it is just as imperative to have an initial champion within the administration and staff.

References

Bauer-Wolf, J. (2018, February 23). Overconfident students, dubious employers. *Inside Higher Education.* Available from https://www.insidehighered.com/news/

2018/02/23/study-students-believe-they-are-prepared-workplace-employers-disagree

Blank, S. (2013). Why the lean start-up changes everything. *Harvard Business Review, 91*(5), 63–72. Available from https://hbr.org/2013/05/why-the-lean-start-up-changes-everything

Drucker, P. F. (1985). *Innovation and entrepreneurship: Practice and principles.* Oxford, UK: Butterworth-Heinemann.

Fisher, J. L., & Koch, J. V. (2008). *Born, not made: The entrepreneurial personality.* Westport, CT: Praeger Publishers.

Florida Institute of Technology. (2018). *Benjamin Scott.* [Faculty and staff profile.] Available from https://web2.fit.edu/faculty/profiles/profile.php?tracks=sbenjamin

Kahneman, D., & Tversky, A. (1979). Prospect theory: An analysis of decision under risk. *Econometrica, 47,* 263–291.

Kauffman Foundation. (2013). *Entrepreneurship education comes of age on campus: A report.* Available from file:///C:/Users/amgol/Downloads/eshipedcomesofage_report.pdf

Kuckertz, A. (2013). Entrepreneurship education: Status quo and prospective developments. *Journal of Entrepreneurship Education, 16,* 59–71. https://ssrn.com/abstract=1862295 or http://dx.doi.org/10.2139/ssrn.1862295

Kuratko, D. (2005). The emergence of entrepreneurship education: Development, trends, and challenges. *Entrepreneurship Theory and Practice, 29,* 577–598.

Lüthje, C., & Franke, N. (2003). The making of an entrepreneur: Testing a model of entrepreneurial intent among engineering students at MIT. *R & D Management, 33,* 135–147.

Mauer, R., Neergaard, H., Linstad, A. K. (2017). Self-efficacy: Conditioning the entrepreneurial mindset. In M. Brännback & A. Carsrud (Eds.), *Revisiting the entrepreneurial mind: International studies in entrepreneurship,* pp. 319-335. Cham, DEU: Springer.

Nobel, C. (2013). Lean start-up strategy not just for start-ups. *Forbes Magazine.* Available from https://www.forbes.com/sites/hbsworkingknowledge/2013/02/25/lean-start-up-strategy-not-just-for-start-ups/#279c93ea2257

Palmer-Noone, L. (2000). Perceived barriers to innovation: First report from a study on innovation in higher education. *Assessment and Accountability Forum, Summer* (2), 7–9.

Ronstadt, R. (1987). The educated entrepreneurs: A new era of entrepreneurial education is beginning. *American Journal of Small Business, 11*(4), 37–53.

Singh, R. (2008). The shortage of academically trained entrepreneurship faculty: Implications, challenges, and opportunities. *Journal of Entrepreneurship Education, 106,* 117–131.

Teller, A. (2016, April 14). *The unexpected benefit of celebrating failure.* Available from https://www.ted.com/talks/astro_teller_the_unexpected_benefit_of_celebrating_failure/transcript?language=en

Tversky, A., & Kahneman, D. (1991). Loss aversion in riskless choice: A reference-dependent model. *The Quarterly Journal of Economics, 106,* 1039–1061.

3

BUILDING AN ENTREPRENEURIAL ECOSYSTEM

Innovate and Flourish

Eugene Giovannini

A dopting an entrepreneurial mindset within our colleges is part of a mission to better serve our students and our communities. However, to spur real and authentic entrepreneurial growth, this mission has to be much larger than a single classroom or campus initiative. It is more than building curriculum and offering courses and programs with *entrepreneurship* in the title. In effect, we as leaders must ask ourselves the following: How do we instill the principles of this practice in every individual, every faculty member, staff person, dean, vice president, and the president? How do we engage our college to think boldly, to challenge what has historically or politically persisted, and perhaps even dive deeper into models that have previously failed? This chapter delves into these questions and offers several examples of advancing entrepreneurial growth through timely and creative responses to challenges and opportunities.

In building an ecosystem, it is the role of the president/CEO to imbue an entrepreneurial mindset as part of the culture. Tools like the National Association for Community College Entrepreneurship's (NAACE's) *Presidents for Entrepreneurship Pledge (PFEP)* help college leaders do just this. Entrepreneurial ecosystems that innovate and thrive can excel only when we leverage assets in new and creative ways and we structure strong support systems to help such ideas flourish. I firmly believe that in entrepreneurship almost anything goes. Wearing the entrepreneurial hat enables you to be imaginative, original, innovative, and even a little outlandish all in the noble pursuit of finding better and more efficient ways to craft new solutions. And, these are solutions you need not only today but also a year, three years, or a decade in the future.

As the former president of GateWay Community College, founding president of Maricopa Corporate College, and now in my role as chancellor of Tarrant County College District (TCCD), these very questions continue to resonate with me at every stage of my professional journey. Each of these positions provided me with vital experiences of building an entrepreneurial mindset and strategy. In this chapter, every story, example, and narrative is shared to help you map your own entrepreneurial ecosystem—from leveraging college and industry assets through incubation programs and building a corporate college model, to the importance of trust and scalability. This is a journey that demands thinking about things in new and different ways—and challenging long-held assumptions. In his book, *Theory of Economic Development*, economist Joseph A. Schumpeter (1934/1982) broke the traditional thought process about business, and, in effect, placed the entrepreneur at the center of all economic progress. Now, decades later, we can learn from Schumpeter's idea—particularly as we draw on our own entrepreneurial destinies as institutions of higher education.

The Tipping Point

The tipping point for me in starting this work began with the creation of the Center for Entrepreneurial Innovation (CEI). In 2002–2003, the Flinn Foundation commissioned a study for the Phoenix area to develop a roadmap for where the state of Arizona should be in the bioscience industry. From this study came recommendations that specifically spoke to entrepreneurship—the need for wet lab and rentable research space and a business incubator for start-ups in varying industry sectors such as technology, energy, biosciences, and software. The goal was not merely to offer a facility, give clients a key, and take a percentage of the equity; it was also about accessing and scaling what the company needed today, tomorrow, and years to come—all with the goal of job creation at its core.

At the time, I was at GateWay Community College, part of the Maricopa Community Colleges system. A funded proposal from the U.S. Department of Commerce's Economic Development Administration (EDA) ultimately resulted in funding from Maricopa Community Colleges, the City of Phoenix, the EDA, and a corporate donation through Blue Cross & Blue Shield of Arizona to help solve and address a regional issue that we hoped would result in enduring, positive economic impact on the city. By engaging in the Flinn Foundation study and listening and responding to the needs of our community, CEI, which was housed on the GateWay Community

College campus, was born. We created an ecosystem of entrepreneurs, an environment that invested in its entrepreneurial community *and* a mindset promoting access, growth, and sustainability. This idea resonated because it represented much more than a real estate deal and was intrinsically driven by programmatic services.

As CEI clients came on board, the program provided more resources to assist entrepreneurs and their businesses than many of them had received before. Services included open-book accounting, monthly/quarterly reviews in partnership with the Maricopa Small Business Development Center (SBDC), an onsite intellectual property attorney, 3D printing capabilities, and a competitive intelligence lab. We relied heavily on executives in residence, in addition to support staff, for general administrative needs, marketing, public relations, and operations. People were important to building CEI as an entrepreneurial ecosystem as well as the culture. From hallway to hallway, to the building's architectural design, we built an environment that inspired innovation.

CEI was an 18,500-square-foot incubator located strategically along the Metro Light Rail with close proximity to the Sky Harbor Airport. Other amenities included 15 fully furnished suites/offices, nearly 10 wet labs with fume hoods, 6 advanced manufacturing spaces, multiple conference rooms and a break room, state-of-the-art presentation technology, Wi-Fi Internet access, 24/7 access and security, a climate-controlled server room, and computer and printer workstations for mentor and affiliate client offices. It was truly a place where ideas grew and the ecosystem thrived because every program and job created was initiated with purpose.

CEI essentially helped in-house and virtual clients and entrepreneurs follow a script to better determine their needs, and the programmatic piece throughout this process was key to ensure businesses felt supported. Today, clients continue to benefit from the "center's proactive business counseling and mentoring as well as its state-of-the-art facility to commercialize their business" (CEI, 2017). CEI serves as a critical example for building an entrepreneurial ecosystem. If you encourage the creation of networks, partnerships, and support *in and around* your entrepreneurs, your people, and your clients—*and* this new mindset and movement for innovative collaboration—you will flourish. With CEI models, it was about developing and serving the businesses. The companies with the best exits were those supported along the way.

Leadership Matters: Follow the Mission

From the Flinn Foundation study and its initial recommendations for Arizona, I learned it was important for the president/CEO to ask *Where does the community college fit? Does the need complement our mission?* I always recommend returning to the college's purpose, mission, and goals. As CEI evolved, GateWay Community College, with its heavy emphasis on biosciences and health care, was deemed an appropriate partnership, match, and opportunity. Problem-solving begins with creating a formula and expectations for leaders within entrepreneurial ecosystems to keep paramount the adoption of laser-focused, mission-centric decision-making. When presidents hit roadblocks, they should go back to the core mission, the overarching reason why they exist. Financial constraints or delays will surface; however, if the concept and ultimate goal connects with your college's mission, the idea will likely prevail.

Sometimes we face uphill battles. In addition to returning to the college's mission, helping people see the vision (internally and externally) is not always easy. Strong leadership must be entrenched within your culture. When building an entrepreneurial ecosystem and responding to community needs and recommendations, your team can help you expand perspectives. You want people around who are emotionally invested in this shared vision. I am fortunate that in each of my ventures, I have been surrounded by people who think critically and outside of the box. When researching and prospecting ideas, thoughts, and opportunities, I have encouraged them to take these concepts and run with them. Approaching this process through a team-oriented and pragmatic lens gives you, an institutional leader, an advantage. As you create coalitions, assess current resources, and build on your leaders' experiences, do not feel you have to re-create what is already at your fingertips.

Trust Matters: The Discovery Triangle

Over the years, I've grown to appreciate the phrase "seeing is believing." If you can show people you can deliver, you will start building trust. When you show you have the capacity to lead by example—whether you (the ecosystem) or the organization—trust *will* thrive. One particular example comes to mind, which occured during my time with CEI when I had the opportunity to work with a group in Phoenix, Arizona, to develop what is known as the Discovery Triangle (Figure 3.1). The Discovery Triangle is a 25-square-mile economic redevelopment area that spans the urban communities of Phoenix, Tempe, and Scottsdale. "The Discovery Triangle is an asset-rich urban region that is primed for redevelopment and reinvestment. Opportunities for creative infill solutions abound and new projects can be launched speedily" (The Triangle, 2017).

When helping to develop this new concept in its initial phase, heavy concentrations of entrepreneurial industry clusters such as biosciences and emerging technology were needed, as well as heightened attention to the proximity of higher education institutions.

Figure 3.1. The Discovery Triangle.

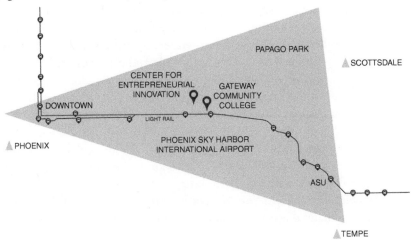

The CEI and GateWay Community College were geographically and strategically located in the middle of the Triangle, creating the anchors for this concept. Along with a motivated and eager team, we mapped the area, highlighting assets, land, warehouses, and potential innovation incubators. We helped recruit businesses to launch here, promoted the effort through local chambers of commerce, and maximized opportunities for the developing light rail system. Trust was critical in making the Discovery Triangle happen. CEI's proven concept, physical space, and support through programmatic offerings helped us leverage and attract other interested parties. People quickly saw results and began to develop trust.

Today, the Discovery Triangle has more than 20 projects either recently completed or under construction across its bandwidth and is assisting the city of Phoenix with its Central Business District expansion. It is also finding ways to foster employment growth for city residents in the Rio Salado redevelopment area. These examples and strategies are key as we see the link between trust and leveraging assets take shape.

Relationships and Sustainability Matter: Bring Value

When building your ecosystem, developing win-win relationships requires you to bring value to the table. We must always return to the community need and recommendations. The ecosystem has to answer the call, and communication is the best way to create a value-added framework or model. Look at all partners and stakeholders and appeal to their mission, desires, and interests. Everyone wants to be part of something successful, and building genuine relationships is centered on consistently evaluating and communicating the value behind the *why*—this creates buy-in and longevity.

The People

You also have to be clear about what you are doing and connect your mission to your actions. In large part, the "seeing is believing" mindset carries through to win-win relationships and ultimately leads to sustainability for your ecosystem. Bringing value to the table, fostering relationships, and demonstrating the investment you've made in your people will reap astounding benefits (Corbin & Schulz, 2017).

For example, at CEI, we had more than 80 pro-bono mentors who gave 2 hours of their time per month. We also had 2 in-house, full-time executives in residence. The latter brought expertise to the table; they knew how to run incubators and were responsible for measuring what clients needed. In short, they were the brains behind the operation, and their role sustained the efforts, initiatives, and goals set forth in the mission. Part-time employees included support staff for the 3D printing lab, intelligence lab, and fabrication lab, and we outsourced an intellectual property attorney. You need a strong technology unit, marketing, and executives in residence to steer the ship. All are critical for nurturing growth, forecasting business needs, and executing a strategic plan for helping in-house and virtual clients succeed.

The Culture

The people who establish the ecosystem are not necessarily the same people who run it. What you can do as a leader in the development stages is to create a culture for sustainability—a culture that promotes no bureaucracy with plenty of space for collaboration, innovation, and connections. At CEI, the executives in residence helped establish a "doing environment" and provided guidance to businesses. They knew each client and encouraged a member-serving-member mentality. The energy, flexibility, fluidity, openness, and think tank culture propelled relationships and sustainability efforts forward, and the center and its clients flourished as a result. While this culture is inherently critical to success, an incubator is not a college, and it is important for us as leaders to adopt this entrepreneurial mindset programmatically as we apply it to our institutions of higher learning.

Ecosystems Matter: The Impact of Scalability

It's good to keep in mind when building an ecosystem that it is not a convenience shop—it is a full-service grocery store! For example, one of the CEI tenants during my tenure was a health care company that started with just 3 or 4 employees and quickly grew to 120 in just over 3 years. They were losing approximately $250,000 a month in revenue and had to close their operations at 2:00 p.m. each day to deliver and ship their samples in time. The company needed to be closer to an airport, which made them consider moving to another city. Rather than simply offering them space, our team built a strong ecosystem around the company and helped them recuperate the $250,000 monthly revenue by repositioning them in an alternative location. The ecosystem supported the company through this initial challenge and continued to stay in the picture. This is a testament to the power of scalability, especially within entrepreneurial ecosystems.

The CEI was also involved in forecasting needs *before* they became needs. This is about thinking ahead, serving the client, and building this strategy into the business plan, all while helping your people get to where they need to be. When developing an ecosystem, ask yourself if you have the components to build and make it scalable or if you are just providing a space/service maybe with a pitch contest here and there. These components can be helpful, but the true hallmark of a successful ecosystem is its sustainability. You must have a strategic vision, plan, and purpose. All companies are uniquely different, and the ecosystem has to accentuate these differentiators.

Whether someone starts all alone in a garage, or has 500,000 square-feet of space and 3,000 employees, the ecosystem has to work with businesses to ensure needs are being met at every stage in the business cycle. This is why mapping and leveraging assets is an indicator for success. Robust ecosystems with strong support programs have the ability to retain their clients longer and with more satisfying results.

Understanding the Structure: Building a Corporate College

As the founding president of Maricopa Corporate College, building a corporate college model provided many valuable insights. This endeavor helped take the Maricopa County Community Colleges District (MCCCD), one of the largest systems in higher education—serving more than 250,000 students—to the next level. The background, resources, and tools provided here serve as a blueprint. Some objectives and goals may look different, depending on your internal and external stakeholders, but the strategy of vetting ideas, defining intentions, evaluating return on investment, establishing community positioning, and garnering philanthropic support are necessary to explore and consider.

Why

Our team knew the corporate college concept was not new and that many community colleges were looking to transition customized business services, contract training, and continuing education into a fiscally driven structure and solution. We also knew the skills gap in the workforce was largely stemming from technology, disaggregation of jobs, the increased pool of untapped talent, disparity of income growth, and geographic mismatch between workers and available jobs. MCCCD offered business services and contract training to approximately 900 companies and municipalities and served more than 42,000 professionals in the Valley of the Sun area. In addition, an estimated 1.8 million new jobs were projected for the state of Arizona over the next 3 decades. Our opportunities and potential were abundant, and the timing to consider a new corporate college model made sense.

The Process, Goals, and Objectives

We decided the mission of the new corporate college would center on delivering high-quality customized training and services to both organizations and businesses in order to advance their strategic initiatives and competitive advantages in the workforce. To accomplish this, we needed to set specific goals and objectives. Because this was a major change for our organization, we wanted to ensure appropriate time was given to the planning process. We used a similar chart provided by Lean Canvas (Figure 3.2) to assess ideas and vet challenges, solutions, metrics, channels, costs, revenue streams, and customers.

We also facilitated workshops and roundtables with key members of district leadership, including the Chancellor's Executive Council, campus presidents, and select vice chancellors and faculty to discuss the ideas, concepts, and strategy tools. One of our top priorities was to solidify a central location for the Maricopa Corporate College facility with accessibility to the light rail system and major freeways. It was important to position the new college with its own identity, and we mapped and assessed square-footage requirements and recommendations while continuing to keep our mission at the forefront.

It was also critical that we determine the organizational structure and include appropriate leadership, support, and program staff. All existing corporate training and business services in the district would be assumed under

Figure 3.2. Chart provided by Lean Canvas.

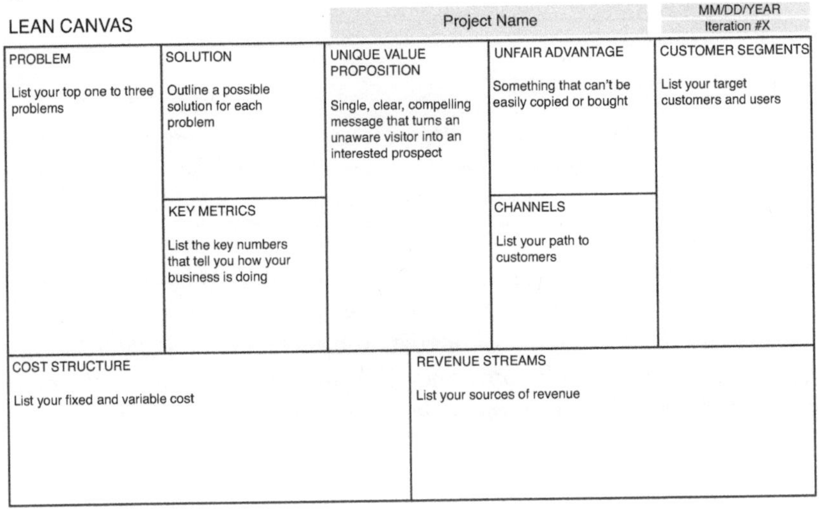

LEAN CANVAS			Project Name		MM/DD/YEAR Iteration #X
PROBLEM List your top one to three problems	SOLUTION Outline a possible solution for each problem	UNIQUE VALUE PROPOSITION Single, clear, compelling message that turns an unaware visitor into an interested prospect		UNFAIR ADVANTAGE Something that can't be easily copied or bought	CUSTOMER SEGMENTS List your target customers and users
	KEY METRICS List the key numbers that tell you how your business is doing			CHANNELS List your path to customers	
COST STRUCTURE List your fixed and variable cost			REVENUE STREAMS List your sources of revenue		

the new college, and non-credit district resources dedicated to similar initiatives were reassigned as applicable. Our team determined government, business, corporate, and industry training needs and linked existing degree and certificate programs where appropriate. It was through these exercises and a comprehensive community survey—designed to make certain the new college was establishing corporate training needs based on constituent needs—that we were able to maximize positioning, philanthropic support, and revenue generation more intentionally.

In addition, a strong link to the Maricopa Community Colleges Foundation was instrumental in accomplishing a holistic plan that included a number of audiences. And, throughout the entire process, a well-organized and executed marketing and communications strategy targeting key internal and external stakeholders remained a high priority. To build a corporate college or any ecosystem leveraging an entrepreneurial mindset, you need externally driven big-picture concepts, clearly identified programmatic needs, and visioning topics/areas to explore in detail. You also need an internally driven roadmap to get there and an organizational mission, as well as information technology, scalability, and team and individual development. It is always important to re-engineer, and re-examine revenue structures to support both current and future operations, investments, and growth projections (Figure 3.3).

As realized in the CEI model and the Discovery Triangle example, it is critical to never lose sight of projecting *future* needs. Your leadership team,

Figure 3.3. Building an entrepreneurial ecosystem.

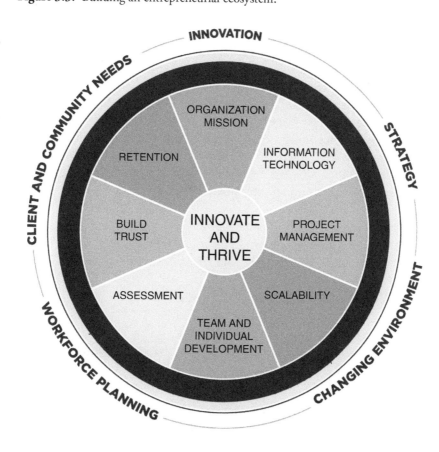

the culture you build, the trust you develop, the relationships you nurture, and how you shape your ecosystem will help sustain and maintain your college's mission. If and when you begin to derail from that, always return to your "why" and the needs of the community.

The Results

The National Association for Community College Entrepreneurship (NACCE) is an organization of educators, administrators, presidents, and entrepreneurs focused on igniting entrepreneurship in communities and campuses. When Maricopa Corporate College was named NACCE's "2015 Entrepreneurial College of the Year," we were recognized for our origination of CEI and the significant impact we made on the Phoenix-area ecosystem through the new corporate college and its mission. By that time, CEI had made a name for itself, helping clients create 145 high-wage jobs with an average annual salary of $56,000. It was also instrumental in generating more than $29 million in total revenue and securing $11 million in grants, awards, and capital investments.

One of the important elements in our ecosystem development was NACCE's *Presidents for Entrepreneurship Pledge* (*PFEP*). This is an action-oriented program for college leaders that encourages strategic initiatives that drive entrepreneurial outcomes. According to NACCE's (2017) quarterly magazine, *Community College Entrepreneurship*, there are five steps for creating economic vitality through entrepreneurship:

1. Form teams to focus on entrepreneurship
2. Connect with entrepreneurs in the community
3. Collaborate with industry in your region
4. Focus on business and job creation
5. Share stories through events and the media

These very steps steered the new corporate college's benchmarking and helped us to capitalize and leverage the right activity and progress forward.

I believe corporate culture is about people and their behaviors. In creating CEI and its culture, we approached it as a business; likewise, Maricopa Corporate College also operated like a business, not a traditional college. In both cases, we capitalized on project management, solutions-driven positioning and decision-making. Results were client-specific, and our mission to encourage stakeholders to work together instead of competing with one another, made for a more efficient use of staff time, eliminated duplication, and promoted better use of technology. You will deliver positive outcomes if you have the right process, people, culture, and objectives in place—and thoroughly execute your plan.

New Approaches to Leveraging Assets

As outlined in this chapter, the CEI, Discovery Triangle, and the corporate college concept are examples of building entrepreneurial ecosystems. You can take similar planning processes and principles to explore concepts and the entrepreneurial mindset approach further. Whether it's in your college, region, or community, what is most important is that you *begin with the end in mind*—a concept introduced by well-known leadership guru and author,

Stephen Covey. *What is the mission of your college, and how can you leverage this to create meaningful impact for the economy? Where do you envision campus and community partnerships? How do these connect to initial needs and recommendations?* The answers to these questions will help launch and propel your ideas forward.

Most recently, in serving as NACCE's board chairman and as the chancellor of TCCD, I continued to see value in tapping new approaches and techniques for entrepreneurship. The tools, questions, and approaches in building and executing a business incubator or corporate college can be adapted to the hub and spokes model (Table 3.1, Figure 3.4). This is an example of what *could* happen and illustrates some ideas for expanding economic vitality through entrepreneurship.

TABLE 3.1
The Hub and Spokes Model

Geographic Region (Sample)	Industry Cluster (Sample)
Fort Worth, TX (The Hub)	Transportation, Aviation, Aerospace, Medical, & Energy
State	Automotive & Health Care
State	Technology & Life Sciences
State	Advanced Manufacturing & Water Technology
State	Agriculture & Telecommunications

Figure 3.4. The hub and spokes model.

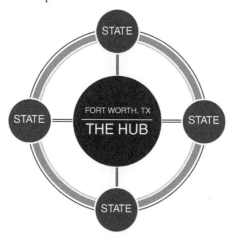

Hub and Spokes Model Defined

The vision for this example is to create physical space and virtual resources for business incubation, boot camps, and makerspaces to be shared across a robust network of community colleges throughout multiple regions. Each region has unique industry clusters and strong partner colleges focused on assisting members in their service areas. In order to close the skills gap, this network idea is structured to focus on innovation and provide opportunities for entrepreneurship to thrive.

As the table and diagram indicate, the proposed hub is Fort Worth, Texas, which supports such industry clusters as transportation, aviation, aerospace, medical, and energy. The selected hub location should have access to training facilities, current models for effective coworking, and resources spanning from strong industry partnerships to a home community college district or campus. The *spokes* connecting and orbiting the hub can include a number of different geographic regions. For purposes of this example, the spokes could be supported and represented by NACCE member institutions to include different states by region. All of these would benefit from the resources the hub provides, and in turn offer their own geographic areas with centralized resources, support, and programmatic offerings.

To elucidate the hub concept in more detail, Fort Worth has a TCC campus located at Alliance Airport, which was an intentional decision made for leveraging existing assets for expanding training programs and resources already in place. As we look at how our colleges can explore and make an entrepreneurial footprint within the region's larger economic ecosystem, you have to think about location. For example, just north of Fort Worth is AllianceTexas. It was developed by Hillwood, a Perot company, and includes 18,000 acres of mixed-use space, is home to over 47,500 employees, 470-plus companies, and has the world's first industrial airport (AllianceTexas, 2017). Due to these advantages and strong job centers, in addition to quality and affordable housing, office and retail space, AllianceTexas is becoming a premier destination for thriving businesses from a variety of industries. Fort Worth and TCC, in this example, are premier options due to these advantages.

Rather than just one county as we saw in the Maricopa example in this chapter, the hub and spokes model encourages a nationwide movement. The strategies, tactics, and development tools discussed in building a corporate college are still relevant as each hub and service region can deploy similar efforts to build a sustainable ecosystem. Whether a small or big concept, think about location, existing resources, and leveraging what is already at your fingertips. We must do this—stretch, grow, and explore beyond the ordinary—our communities need us.

Takeaways

I sometimes refer to spurring entrepreneurial growth as an experience. The table is set, your guests are seated, and entrepreneurship is on the menu. Whether it is your first time or you are highly experienced, it is likely you will taste something new. It is with this mindset that I encourage community college leaders to keep this curiosity alive and active, to engage and operate through a lens of entrepreneurial discovery, and to think big and boldly in taking your ecosystems to the next levels.

I personally believe the future of America will be built around small businesses. This is why providing opportunities to potential employees to fill the 6.2 million jobs that need skilled workers *today* is of the essence. And, it is important to remember the 10 million jobs created over the *next* 10 years will need a skilled and vibrant workforce, too. Whether through the CEI, the Discovery Triangle, building a corporate college, or establishing a hub and spokes model, making impact across multiple sectors, organizational mission, job creation, and promoting a shared vision was—and continues to remain—a priority. This chapter provided a number of suggestions for next steps. My hope is that these will help guide you through *your* story and opportunities. Let the following list of key takeaways ignite a new way of thinking onward and upward, and let them be your call to action:

- Be fearless in taking a reality check of your community and addressing what you find. Speak up and address how the community college fits and answers the call.
- Leverage your institution's reputation and maximize partnerships and resources through new and different collaboration strategies. Do not re-create what is already at your fingertips.
- Ecosystems are bundles of different accelerators, incubators, fab labs, components, and other entities. Go beyond just real estate and equity and consider the support and programmatic structures it will take to ensure scalability for your clients.
- Challenge assumptions and think critically about your actions. Do the right things right, and do not be too worried about getting there quickly—meaningless and unintentional activity is not progress.
- Use listening as your mapping tool. Be mindful about what you are hearing and what is actual reality. It is always important to connect back to your college's mission. If the two are ever disjointed, find the link.
- Run your ecosystem, whether it's an incubator or corporate college, like a business. Create and develop assessments, tools, benchmarks,

goals, and objectives. The investment in your people and your culture is critical.

- Embrace and adopt an entrepreneurial mindset; once you plant the seeds, cultivate them and you will see them grow. Timing is everything.

References

AllianceTexas. (2017). *Home page*. Available from http://alliancetexas.com

Center for Entrepreneurial Innovation (CEI). (2017). *About CEI*. Available from https://www.ceigateway.com/about/

Corbin, R., & Schulz, A. (2017, October 7). Community colleges and the creation of entrepreneurial ecosystems. *Entrepreneur.com*. Available from http://www.entrepreneur.com

National Association for Community College Entrepreneurship (NACCE). (2017, Summer/Fall). *What is the presidents for entrepreneurship pledge?* Available from http://www.nacce.com

Schumpeter, Joseph A. (1982). *The theory of economic development: An inquiry into profits, capital, credit, interest, and the business cycle*. New York, NY: Taylor and Francis. Original work published 1934.

The Triangle. (2017). *The region*. Available from http://www.discoverytriangle.org/the-triangle.html

4

ENTREPRENEURSHIP AND WORKFORCE DEVELOPMENT

Christopher Mullin and Doan Winkel

Entrepreneurship has always been the backbone of the American economy. While we have yet to see entrepreneurship activity return to the levels of the 1970s to the early 2000s, promising research from the Kauffman Foundation shows that business start-up activity is continuing a three-year upward trend (Fairlie, Reedy, Morelix, & Russell, 2016). Combined with the United States' leading position as the most promising environment for cultivating entrepreneurship, this is encouraging news for our future workforce (Acs, Szerb, & Lloyd, 2017). Research conducted under the banner of the Global Entrepreneurship Monitor found that the level of entrepreneurship activity in a country explains 70% of the difference in economic growth. The research further found that all nations with high levels of entrepreneurial activity have above average rates of economic growth. We know that economic growth is dependent on entrepreneurial activity, which is dependent on cultural attitudes (Landes, 1998). The United States is at a critical crossroads of workforce development and entrepreneurship; we can shift our focus toward job creation and entrepreneurship, or we can be left behind on the global stage (Consortium for Entrepreneurship Education, 2009). As this report states,

> Fostering an entrepreneurial mindset is essential to our future success, and teaching entrepreneurial skills to all learners (whether or not they eventually start a business) is a no-lose proposition for the U.S. economy. . . . Using workforce development resources to create a pipeline of future entrepreneurs in our schools can yield dividends for individuals, businesses, and society as a whole. (Consortium for Entrepreneurship Education, 2009)

Critical to this nexus of entrepreneurship and workforce development in America is the community college infrastructure being developed across the country. As Tom Vander Ark (2018) notes in a recent *Forbes* column, "For individuals, the right kind of education can boost employability. For communities, educational attainment correlates with better social, economic and personal outcomes for citizens." Community colleges provide that "right kind of education" for students to boost their employability because they are the primary providers of a community workforce that aligns with regional employment and economic development needs (Myran & Ivery, 2013). Weaving entrepreneurship into the fabric of community college education only strengthens the workforce development potential of these institutions.

Within most community colleges, entrepreneurship is viewed as a substantive curriculum—something that should be a critical component of every student's experience during his or her tenure. Often, college faculty work to develop courses in the business area of their instructional unit. We see courses in areas vital to preparing entrepreneurs to think and act like an entrepreneur. Courses are teaching students an entrepreneurial mindset and the hard skills necessary to start and grow a business, such as marketing, computer applications, leadership and management, and entrepreneurship and innovation (Kelley, Singer, & Herrington, 2016). In some cases, these courses are combined with marketing programs out of which students develop their ideas to promote business activities.

This focus on entrepreneurship is evolving in response to the new economic realities facing many community colleges. Despite the economic recovery and growth since the Great Recession of 2008–2009, the up-to-date news trumpeted by the media of the "tightening of the labor market" (U.S. Bureau of Labor Statistics, 2015), in many communities, the number of sustainable wage jobs, particularly for those without four-year degrees, is still very low. In addition, much of the employment that existed within these communities is threatened by a combination of technical change and the outsourcing of work overseas. As a result, the fundamental mission of the community college—to provide skills for individuals to obtain work in their communities—is challenged. Community colleges have historically been exceedingly good at responding to the demands of employers, but what if that demand is not present? Can a focus on training students for entrepreneurship address the new economic reality facing America?

Trends to Consider

Community college service areas cover every square inch of America. Nearly two-thirds of these service areas in rural communities with fewer than 2,500 full-time students enrolled. While community college constitutes the final opportunity for advancement at the end of an educational continuum for most local residents, the endpoint is permeable. This permeability—or open-access approach to enrollment—serves as a commitment to the latent potential within students. It allows for businesses to continue growing through human capital development, and it allows for communities to reshape themselves when necessary, although this may not be happening enough.

We will present trends that suggest that although more Americans are becoming more educated, and with knowledge becoming more specialized, access to occupations remains unequally distributed, and the number of new firms are declining. One powerful solution to these problems can come from localized workforce development, and the human capital for the development must be local community colleges. Faced with this situation, it is necessary for community college staff to consider how their institution can create economic activities in their communities through an aggressive workforce development strategy that views entrepreneurial activity as essential to the well-being of their students and their community. This can take many forms of business incubators, including applied research centers to help local industry, small business assistance centers, innovation funders, and makerspaces, to name a few.

A Greater Percentage of Americans Have Completed College

Figure 4.1 illustrates what we know but do not often verbalize: America's education system has continuously improved, with a greater number of students graduating from high school and college. The increase in education attainment has a variety of factors, including demographics. However, the variability of attainment across counties is equally as important as the overall increase, while receiving much less attention. For example, in Florida, educational attainment rates varied between counties, from 12% to 55% (Lumina Foundation, 2017). Research by labor market economists and others have shown that as one's educational attainment increases, so does one's income (Mullin, Baime, &, Honeyman, 2015). We also know that the wage premium for a college degree has also increased (Carnevale & Rose, 2011), and that certain degree programs result in higher postcollege wages (Carnevale, Smith & Strohl, 2010).

A recent study by Levine and Rubinstein (2015) found that entrepreneurs who owned incorporated businesses earned 36% more than their salaried counterparts. Another study by Manso (2016) found that individuals who had been self-employed at one point in their career had higher career earnings when compared to similar workers who hadn't. As students are

Figure 4.1. School completed by people 25 years of age and older: Selected years 1964–2017.

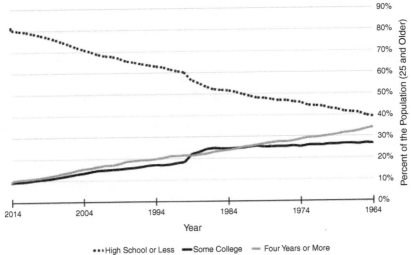

Source: Author's analysis of United States Census Bureau, 2017.

generally attaining greater education degrees, if they learn more about entrepreneurship, and can apply those skills during their career path, it is reasonable to expect they will realize higher career earnings.

We must not only own and celebrate the positive increase in educational attainment but also acknowledge that the success we have made in the aggregate is not evenly distributed across all Americans. Educational attainment is related to, but different from, college completion in that annual completion numbers are of awards given, and not a reflection of a percent of a population. Because of their relatedness, it is also not surprising to see the number of college certificates and degrees increase (Figure 4.2).

Public opinion of the need for a college credential in the workforce tends to increase during economic downturns, only to decrease during times of economic advancement (Immerwahr & Johnson, 2007). This instability in opinion offers one insight: individual perceptions can change, and in more and more cases, they need to. For instance, no longer can the shade tree mechanic open a shop and it be as viable as it may have been in the past. Advancements in automobiles require more advanced knowledge and the ability to operate sophisticated equipment—much of which requires education and training. On a broader scale, the coming Fourth Industrial Revolution is creating opportunities in fields such as advanced robotics, artificial intelligence, autonomous transport, machine learning, and genomics (Schwab, 2015).

Figure 4.2. Degrees/certificates conferred by postsecondary institutions: 1995–1996 through 2015–2016.

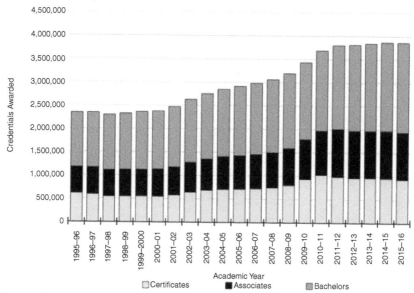

Source: Author's analysis of National Center of Education Statistics, 2016. Table 318.40.

Additionally, the gig economy is transforming the American workforce, with a growing majority of organizations indicating they will use contingent workers by 2020 (Ernst & Young, n.d.). This nascent class of worker will need to exhibit an entrepreneurial mindset and skill set to survive (Mulcahy, 2016). Community colleges are perfectly poised to provide entrepreneurship training to these freelance and contingent workers, and thus will play a leadership role in aligning community ecosystems to leverage this emerging workforce. Developments like these will transform the way we work. The top skills necessary for employment in the next 10 years overlap directly with the skills necessary to think and act entrepreneurially (World Economic Forum, 2016).

Given these shifts, it is educationally and economically imperative to expand our students' understanding of the range of potential occupations to support the localized creation of businesses that offer a greater range of opportunities.

Geographic Access to All Occupations Is Not a Reality

Economists have developed something called the location quotient to show how prevalent an occupation is relative to the national average. The average

Figure 4.3. Location quotient of computer hardware engineers by area, May 2016.

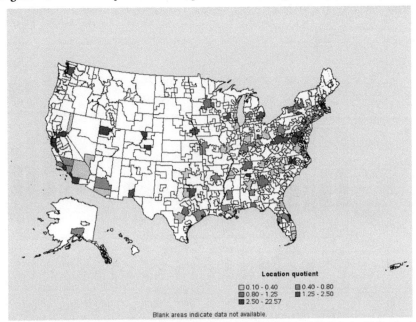

Source: Map by the Office of Economic Studies, U.S. Department of Labor. U.S. Bureau of Labor Statistics, 2018. Available from www.bls.gov/oes/current/map_changer.htm

is numerically expressed as 1, so 1.25 equates to an occupation being 125% more prevalent in a particular area than the national average. What is more interesting than the indicator itself is the vast emptiness of occupations when mapped across the country. Figure 4.3 is a map downloaded from the U.S. Department of Labor website that shows the location quotient for computer hardware engineers, which serves as just one of countless examples.

What Figure 4.3 shows is that there is not a job market for computer hardware engineers in many parts of the country. This graph is nearly identical for many skilled and technical occupations. Furthermore, if high-paying occupations are centered in certain parts of the country, then it would follow that America's financial fabric is diverse. This fact is reinforced in Figure 4.4, which depicts the distribution of average wages by county.

The questions for each community is as follows: How can community colleges support students who have an interest in low-to-no density occupations in their community? How can their community strategically identify economic development plans that bring new opportunities and diversify a

Figure 4.4. Distribution of average weekly wage, by wage range for all counties, 2017.

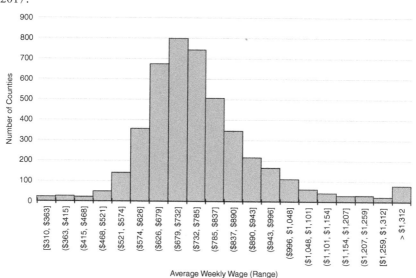

Source: U.S. Department of Labor (n.d.). Author's analysis of Quarterly Census of Employment and Wages (QCEW).

community's business environment? Entrepreneurship can be that catalyst. If community colleges continue to invest in entrepreneurship training and incubation, the surrounding communities should see an increase in entrepreneurial activity, which should lead to economic growth and greater job creation (Badal, 2010).

Communities do not seem to be diversifying their business environments, however. In fact, fewer firms are being created. A trend of consistent decline has existed since 1977 (Figure 4.5).

An increasing number of new firms employ 250 people or more, suggesting that small to mid-sized businesses are not as prevalent as they once were. Compounding matters is that even when new businesses start, half of all establishments close within five years (U.S. Bureau of Labor Statistics, 2017). Why? What do community colleges need to do to reverse this trend?

Moving Forward

It is essential for community college leaders and champions to understand the local economy in which they are a critical player, and to specifically build

Figure 4.5. Start-up density 1977–2016.

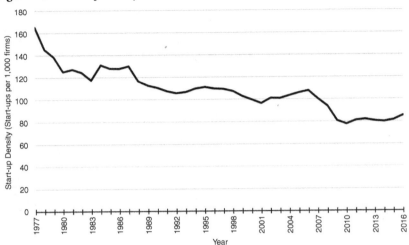

Note. An establishment is a single physical location, whereas a firm represents either one establishment or a combination of establishments (Akbar, Talan, & Clayton, 2016).
Source: Author's analysis of the Kauffman Index of Startup Activity data file. Kauffman Foundation, 2018. Available from www.kauffman.org/kauffman-index/about/archive-and-data

programs and opportunities for business activity within their respective communities. The trends discussed here suggest that although more Americans are becoming more educated, knowledge is becoming more specialized, and access to occupations remains unequally distributed. If we hope to ensure that all Americans have a chance at a living wage in a viable community, the answer has to come from the nexus of entrepreneurship education and localized workforce development, and the human capital for the development must be local community colleges.

Coupled with these trends has been the growing research, which ties many of the characteristics of student success at the workplace to the characteristics of entrepreneurial behavior. Students who can take advantage of situations, who learn to market themselves, and who are willing to take risks become successful in school as well as in the workforce. According to research conducted by the World Economic Forum (2016), the top 10 skills most desired by employers by 2020 are a laundry list of entrepreneurial competencies. From complex problem-solving and creativity, to emotional intelligence and negotiation, the skills employees need to succeed can be developed in entrepreneurial classrooms of community colleges across the nation. These institutions hold the promise of tomorrow in their ability to build curriculum and programming around the intersection of entrepreneurship and workforce development.

Preparing Students for the Gig Economy

Preparation of college students to enter the gig economy is imperative if student success is measured not only by degree attainment but also by financial security in life. A 2018 study commissioned by Nation1099 found:

> Employment in general is undergoing dramatic changes, often summarized as the future of work or Workforce 2.0. Anyone following workforce trends will have seen eye-popping numbers about the gig economy along the lines of one third of all workers are freelancers or half of us will be in the gig economy by 2020. (McGuire, 2018)

Gig Economy Statistics

Several statistics demonstrate the impact of the gig economy:

- *86% of professional freelancers choose freelancing* (Field Nation, 2016)
- *35% of the U.S. workforce—55 million people—freelanced in 2016* (Upwork Global, Inc., 2016)
- *Update: 36% of the U.S. workforce—57.3 million people—freelanced in 2017* (Upwork Global, Inc., 2016)
- *19.8% of full-time independents earn more than $100,000* (MBO Partners, 2017b)
- *By 2027, more than half of American workers—58%—will have had some experience as independent contractors* (MBO Partners, 2017a)
- *20% of organizations globally with more than 1,000 employees have a workforce that is made up of 30% or more contingent workers* (Ernst & Young, 2017)
- *7.6 million Americans will be working in the on-demand economy regularly by 2020* (Intuit, 2015)
- *94% of workers are open to nontraditional forms of work* (Manpower Group, 2017)
- *20% to 30% of the working-age population in the United States and the European Union engage in independent work* (McKinsey Global Institute, 2016)

The American Association of Community Colleges (AACC) described the gig movement, highlighting several community colleges that are successfully preparing students for the gig economy (Guth, 2016). Emphasizing "entrepreneurial spirit," Guth cited specific examples of community college students solving problems by creating solutions through workforce development programs. In one case, a student created a tech start-up, Vitris Wireless, to help people find solutions to frustrating technology problems with an easy-to-use app. The student acknowledged that Bucks County Community College (BCCC) in Newtown, Pennsylvania, helped him learn the money management and organizational skills that are crucial for entrepreneurs to thrive in the gig economy. National Association for Community College Entrepreneurship (NACCE) President and CEO Rebecca Corbin, whom Guth interviewed for the article, noted, "With young people, it's preparing them for the gig economy, even if not everyone is going to be the next founder of Facebook."

Makerspaces and fab labs have come to play a critical role by providing equipment and opportunities to collaborate. At Northampton Community College (NCC) in Bethlehem Township, Pennsylvania, Jeff Boerner, an entrepreneur with a passion for tinkering, created a fab lab, acquiring unused space and donated equipment. In exchange for use of the equipment, fab lab users were required to teach a course to others. Boerner has collaborated with Corbin and NACCE to highlight his story, which includes leveraging local assets, including nearby Nazareth, Pennsylvania, home of Martin Guitar. The result: a signature guitar-making course at NCC and the perfect complement for a musician's gig lifestyle.

It is essential for community colleges to understand the local economy and its needs, specifically to build programs and create opportunities for business activity within the community. There is growing research that ties many of the characteristics of student success in the workplace to the characteristics of entrepreneurial behavior. Students who can take advantage of situations, who learn to market themselves, and who are willing to take risks, become successful in school as well as at work. In an almost paradoxical situation, today's entrepreneur is not the stand-alone hero of Ayn Rand novels, but a rock climber who takes advantage of the situations and networks with others to achieve goals.

Takeaways

- Community colleges should teach entrepreneurial skills to all students to contribute to creating a more entrepreneurial workforce.
- Community colleges have the opportunity to take the lead in providing entrepreneurship training to the gig economy workforce.
- Harness the potential of the gig economy by attracting and training the super temps. The term *super temps* is used to describe top managers and professionals—from lawyers to CFOs and consultants—who choose to pursue project-based careers independent of any major company (Miller & Miller, 2012).

- Employers want employees who exhibit an entrepreneurial mindset and skill set. High schools and four-year universities are not providing this practical education, which provides an opportunity for community colleges.
- Leverage your institution's position in the local community to modernize workforce development through entrepreneurship education initiatives.
- Use workforce development resources to teach students entrepreneurial skills.

References

Acs, Z. J., Szerb, L., & Lloyd, A. (2017). *Global entrepreneurship and development index*. New York, NY: Springer.

Akbar, S., Talan, D. M., & Clayton, R. L. (2016, Nov.). Establishment, firm, or enterprise: Does the unit of analysis matter? *Monthly Labor Review*. Available from https://www.bls.gov/opub/mlr/2016/article/establishment-firm-or-enterprise.htm

Badal, S. (2010). *Entrepreneurship and job creation: Leveraging the relationship*. Gallup, Inc. Available from https://kipdf.com/entrepreneurship-and-job-creation_5ad72e667f8b9adc0a8b45b9.html.

Carnevale, A., & Rose, S. (2011). *The undereducated American*. Washington DC: Georgetown University Center on Education and the Workforce.

Carnevale, A., Smith, N., & Strohl, J. (2010, June). *Help wanted: Projections of jobs and education requirements through 2018*. Washington DC: Georgetown University, Center for Education and the Workforce. Available from https://cew.georgetown.edu/cew-reports/help-wanted/

Consortium for Entrepreneurship Education. (2009). *Think entrepreneurs: A call to action. Integrating entrepreneurship into the public workforce system throughout America.* Available from https://wdr.doleta.gov/research/FullText_Documents/Think%20Entrepreneurs%20A%20Call%20to%20Action%20-%20Integrating%20Entrepreneurship%20into%20the%20Public%20Workforce%20System%20Throughout%20America.pdf

Ernst & Young. (n.d.). *The gig economy: Transforming the workforce.* Available from http://www.ey.com/gl/en/services/people-advisory-services/the-gig-economy-transforming-the-workforce_old

Ernst & Young. (2017). *Global contingent workforce study.* Available from https://gigeconomy.ey.com

Fairlie, R. W., Reedy, E. J., Morelix, A., & Russell, J. (2016). *The Kauffman Index startup activity: National trends.* The Kauffman Foundation. Available from https://www.kauffman.org/kauffman-index

Field Nation. (2016). *The 2016 Field Nation freelancer study: The changing face of the new blended workforce.* Available from https://fieldnation.com/wp-content/uploads/2017/03/The_2016_Field_Nation_Freelancer_Study_R1V1__1_-2.pdf

Guth, D. (2016, December 5). Creating the entrepreneurial mindset. *Community College Daily*. Washington DC. Available from http://ccdaily.com/2016/12/creating-the-entrepreneurial-mindset/

Immerwahr, J., & Johnson, J. (2007). *Squeeze play: How parents and the public look at higher education today.* (National Center Report #07-4.) San Jose, CA: National Center for Public Policy and Higher Education.

Intuit. (2015). *Intuit forecast: 7.6 million people in on-demand economy by 2020.* Available from https://investors.intuit.com/press-releases/press-release-details/2015/intuit-forecast-76-million-people-in-on-demand-economy-by-2020/default.aspx

Kauffman Foundation. 2018. *Archive and data.* Available from https://www.kauffman.org/kauffman-index/about/archive-and-data

Kelley, D., Singer, S., & Harrington, M. (2016). Global entrepreneurship monitor global report 2015/2016. Global Entrepreneurship Research Association. Available from http://www.gemconsortium.org/report/49480

Landes, David S. (1998). *The wealth and poverty of nations: Why are some so rich and others so poor?* New York, NY: W.H. Norton & Company.

Levine, R., & Rubinstein, Y. (2015). *Smart and illicit: Who becomes an entrepreneur and do they earn more?* Available from https://web.archive.org/web/20160222033032/http://faculty.haas.berkeley.edu/ross_levine/Papers/smart_and_illicit_24sep2015.pdf

Lumina Foundation. (2017). *A stronger nation.* Available from http://strongernation.luminafoundation.org/report/2018/#nation

Manpower Group. (2017). *#GigResponsibly: The rise of nextgen work.* Available from http://www.manpowergroup.co.uk/the-word-on-work/gig-responsibly/

Manso, G. (2016). Experimentation and the returns to entrepreneurship. *The Review of Financial Studies, 29*(9), 2319–2340.

MBO Partners. (2017a). *Looking forward: What will the independent workforce look like in 2027?* Available from https://www.mbopartners.com/future-of-work

MBO Partners. (2017b). *MBO partners state of independence in America 2018.* Available from https://www.mbopartners.com/state-of-independence

McGuire, R. (2018, January). *Ulitmate guide to gig economy data: A summary of every freelance survey we can find.* Available from http://nation1099.com/gig-economy-data-freelancer-study/

McKinsey Global Institute. (2016). *Independent work: Choice, necessity, and the gig economy.* Available from https://www.mckinsey.com/featured-insights/employment-and-growth/independent-work-choice-necessity-and-the-gig-economy

Miller, J. G., & Miller, M. (2012, May). The rise of the supertemp. *Harvard Business Review.* Available from https://hbr.org/2012/05/the-rise-of-the-supertemp

Mulcahy, D. (2016, October 27). Who wins in the gig economy, and who loses. *Harvard Business Review.* Available from https://hbr.org/2016/10/who-wins-in-the-gig-economy-and-who-loses

Mullin, C. M., Baime, D. S., & Honeyman, D. S. (2015). *Community college finance: A guide for institutional leaders.* Hoboken, NJ: Wiley.

Myran, G., & Ivery, C. L. (2013). The employability gap and the community college role in workforce development. *New Directions for Community Colleges, 162,* 45–53.

Nation1099. (2018). The career freelancer status report: Results from the Nation1099 survey, 2018. Available from https://nation1099.com/freelance-survey/

National Center for Education Statistics. (2016). *Digest of Education Statistics,* Table 318.40. Available from https://nces.ed.gov/programs/digest/current_tables.asp

Schwab, K. (2015, December 12). The Fourth Industrial Revolution: What it means and how to respond. *Foreign Affairs.* Available from https://www.foreignaffairs.com/articles/2015-12-12/fourth-industrial-revolution

U.S. Bureau of Labor Statistics. (2014). Characteristics of minimum wage workers, 2013. *BLS Reports* [Report 1048]. Available from https://www.bls.gov/opub/reports/minimum-wage/archive/minimumwageworkers_2013.pdf

U.S. Bureau of Labor Statistics. (2017). Table 7. Survival of private sector establishments by opening year. Available from https://www.bls.gov/bdm/bdmage.htm#TOTAL

U.S. Bureau of Labor Statistics. (2018). *Occupational Employment Statistics, May 2017, OES maps. Employment of architecture and engineering occupations, by state, May 2017.* Available from https://www.bls.gov/oes/current/map_changer.htm

U.S. Census Bureau. (2017). *CPS historical times series tables.* Available from https://www.census.gov/data/tables/time-series/demo/educational-attainment/cps-historical-time-series.html

U.S. Department of Labor. (n.d.). *Quarterly census of employment and wages.* Available from https://www.bls.gov/cew/

Upwork Global, Inc. (2016). *Freelancing in America.* Available from https://www.upwork.com/i/freelancing-in-america/2016/

Vander Ark, Tom. (2018 April 3). Credentialing America: How impact investing can help. *Forbes.* Available from https://www.forbes.com/sites/tomvanderark/2018/04/03/credentialing-america-how-impact-investing-can-help/#4212c8ad2e1e

World Economic Forum. (2016, January). *The future of jobs: Employment, skills and workforce strategy for the Fourth Industrial Revolution.* Global Challenge Insight report. Available from http://www3.weforum.org/docs/WEF_Future_of_Jobs.pdf

5

INVISIBLE OPPORTUNITIES

How Collaboration Supports the Growth
of an Urban Entrepreneurial Ecosystem

Steven Tello

This chapter examines the roles played by the University of Massachusetts Lowell (UMass Lowell); Middlesex Community College; the Deshpande Foundation; and other civic, business, and community partners in supporting the emergence of a sustainable, entrepreneurial ecosystem in the postindustrial mill city of Lowell, Massachusetts. We underscore the challenges we faced in attracting entrepreneurs, talent, and capital to a multi-ethnic city recovering from the Great Recession of 2008 while the entrepreneurial tech hub of Boston, Massachusetts, was beginning to boom only 40 miles south of Lowell.

We use Isenberg's domains of entrepreneurial ecosystems to frame Lowell's story, sharing an approach to building an ecosystem that can be replicated in other midsize cities across the country. This framework examines culture, leadership and policies, infrastructure, human capital, finance, and venture capital support.

We close by sharing several important personal reflections on our journey:

1. Allow faculty and staff time to explore new initiatives.
2. Early collisions support learning and establish longer term relationships.
3. Our institutions serve important convening functions when establishing new initiatives and relationships.
4. Open your doors to others.
5. Be open to new models.
6. Don't overlook invisible opportunities.

About Lowell and UMass Lowell

Lowell, Massachusetts, is located 35 miles north of the Boston-Cambridge life science supercluster. However, for many years, the community and economy of Lowell did not directly benefit from the innovation and investment taking place a short distance away in the hub of New England. Lowell, a postindustrial mill town, had seen several of its own boom and bust cycles, the first few associated with the textile industry and later with the region's electronics and computing industry. The most recent boom ended in the mid-1980s, as two major global computer companies in the region, Wang and Digital Equipment Corporation, shut down, taking thousands of jobs and affecting both former employees and the supply chain in the region. While many have heard of the greater Boston technology corridor formed around Route 128 in the 1970s, and the life science supercluster formed around Boston-Cambridge in this century, fewer have ventured further north to the older mill cities of Lowell, Lawrence, and Haverhill. While all 3 cities are located within a 40-minute commuter rail or car ride south to Boston, they were not able to leverage the technology booms of the 1970s or 2000s in any lasting manner. This chapter shares our efforts to leverage university and community resources in a way that supports the growth of a sustainable entrepreneurship ecosystem outside the established technology hub of New England.

The city of Lowell has a population of approximately 120,000. The first planned textile mill community in the United States was established in Lowell in the mid-1800s. For decades, well into the 1940s, the textile industry and the mill culture dominated the city and the surrounding communities lined on the Merrimack River.

While the initial textile mill workforce comprised primarily the daughters of the region's farming families—the original mill girls—over time, successive waves of immigrants from Ireland, Canada, Greece, Poland, Portugal, and other regions supplanted and replaced the local Yankee workforce, bringing a distinct mix of culture and community to the city of Lowell.

The city still has a very high immigrant population: 42% of the households in Lowell speak English as a second language, and 28.5% of the city's residents are foreign born. Lowell hosts the second largest Cambodian population in the United States, after Long Beach, California. Twenty-one percent of the city's population is of Asian descent, 18% is Hispanic, 7% is Black or African American, and 50% is White (United States Census Bureau, 2015). The city is diverse and celebrates this diverse cultural heritage through events and celebrations. Lowell hosts the largest free outdoor folk festival in the country every July, and the music diversity reflects the many immigrant groups in the city. The Lowell Folk Festival is complemented by numerous cultural events throughout the year, each celebrating members of the respective ethnic groups that call Lowell their home.

Training the Workforce, Educating the Citizens

In the period from 1830 to 1900, the population of Lowell grew significantly, and the needs of the textile industry grew as well. The forerunner institutes to UMass Lowell were created in response to these needs. The Lowell Normal School was founded in 1894 to provide teacher training to women in the region, so they could in turn teach the booming population of children in the area.

Three years later, in 1897 in another part of town, the Lowell Textile Institute was founded to train the technicians and engineers needed to serve the textile mills. Lowell Textile Institute became Lowell Technological Institute in 1953, growing its academic programs and adding electronics technology to the mix. Similarly, Lowell Normal School eventually became the Lowell State College, adding the study of liberal arts and the humanities. These two schools merged into the University of Lowell in 1975 and then joined the University of Massachusetts system in 1991. Throughout its history, the programs offered at UMass Lowell have focused on providing a professional education that contributes to the support and growth of the workforce in the region.

Today, the university is composed of 6 colleges and serves 18,300 students across undergraduate, graduate, and continuing education programs. The six colleges include:

1. College of Education
2. College of Fine Arts, Humanities and Social Sciences
3. Francis College of Engineering
4. Kennedy College of Sciences
5. Manning School of Business
6. Zuckerburg College of Health Sciences

True to its original roots, these six colleges are clearly focused on providing graduates with professional education that meets the workforce needs of the region and beyond. College of Education graduates serve as teachers, principals, and superintendents across Massachusetts and New England.

Engineering graduates work in and lead major regional companies, including Raytheon, Boston Scientific, Kronos, and others. Science graduates work in the leading life science companies, serve as weather forecasters, and lead in robotics and computer science innovations and companies.

Programs like Sound Recording Technology, Community Social Psychology and Criminal Justice in the College of Fine Arts, Humanities and Social Sciences, provide graduates with both a humanities perspective and an applied professional education. In fact, a survey of 2017 UMass Lowell graduates found that 95% of respondents had secured employment or had been accepted to graduate school (www.uml.edu/News/news-articles/2017/sun-grads-jobs.aspx).

In addition to meeting regional workforce needs, the professional focus of UMass Lowell education reflects the professional aspirations of the students (and their families). In 2016, 23% of the undergraduate student body was comprised of first-generation college students, the first in their families to attend college (Meehan, 2017).

A significant percentage of the undergraduate student body works 20 hours or more per week while attending classes. This is not a surprise given the cultural and economic diversity of Lowell and the region. While the high immigrant population in the city contributes to its cultural diversity, it also presents some economic challenges as recent immigrants and their first-generation children work to pursue professional and economic aspirations. Median household income in the city is $48,000, compared to a national median household income of $53,657. Similarly, per capita income in Lowell is $22,637 compared to $28,889 at the national level (Neighborhood Scout, 2017). Today's UMass Lowell students, like generations of predecessors, view their university education as the pathway to a professional career and better paying jobs.

These details are important in understanding the nature of the aspirations of these students and an education at UMass Lowell. They also suggest the challenge one faces in building an entrepreneurial ecosystem in a community where a paying job has more value than a risky start-up venture. UMass Lowell students tend not to think of entrepreneurship as a professional career option, focusing instead on concrete job opportunities in established companies. However, in many respects, these students are quite entrepreneurial. They are hands-on (we offer co-op and experiential education programs). They like to build things (8,000 square-feet of makerspace). They know how to gather the resources needed to acquire an education and life's necessities. They know how to "boot strap" life, and this is an important skill for any entrepreneur. One challenge faced in building the Lowell entrepreneurial ecosystem was to bring students along.

Building an Entrepreneurial Ecosystem

Before going further, it is important to define the term *entrepreneurial ecosystem*. Isenberg suggests that an entrepreneurial ecosystem is a "metaphor for fostering entrepreneurship as an economic development strategy" (Isenberg, 2014). He goes on to identify six domains that support the emergence and sustainability of entrepreneurial ecosystems (Figure 5.1).

This definition suggests that the development of an entrepreneurial ecosystem is a shared responsibility that requires the engagement and support of multiple institutions and organizations—higher education, government, banking and finance, cultural and neighborhood groups, business and others. Isenberg also reminds us that each entrepreneurial ecosystem is unique, reflecting the community, the region, and the institutions in which it emerges—the ecosystem is context sensitive.

Figure 5.1. Isenberg's six domains of an entrepreneurship ecosystem.

Note. Isenberg, Daniel (2011). Introducing the entrepreneurship ecosystem: Four defining characteristics. *Forbes.* Available from www.forbes.com/sites/danisenberg/2011/05/25/introducing-the-entrepreneurship-ecosystem-fourdefining-characteristics/#25db31785fe8; www.nps.gov/lowe/learn/photosmultimedia/decline.htm

This perspective of an entrepreneurial ecosystem has important implications for any community or region that aspires to leverage entrepreneurship as an economic development strategy. It clearly establishes a shared and collaborative process, with multiple players from different domains, each bringing different types of resources to the ecosystem. It runs counter to the traditional university technology transfer model, which has too often focused on pushing academic innovation into the market place, without necessarily understanding context and culture. It also suggests that top-down initiatives, without bottom-up support and broader business and community engagement, will have limited success in building an ecosystem. In short, an entrepreneurial ecosystem is built by the people and organizations in a region that will benefit from its success.

Lowell's Entrepreneurial Ecosystem

Today, Lowell supports a thriving entrepreneurial ecosystem that engages a myriad of stakeholders: UMass Lowell and National Association for Community College Entrepreneurship (NACCE) member Middlesex Community College, the Lowell Development Finance Corporation, the Lowell Plan, the Deshpande Foundation's EforAll, the region's banks, commercial real estate developers, regional angel investor groups, nonprofit community agencies like Community Teamwork and the Coalition for a Better Acre, local small businesses, regional corporations, and numerous technology and non-tech start-up entrepreneurs. These stakeholders bring unique resources and perspectives to the ecosystem that support its growth.

- The university operates 34,000 square-feet of technology start-up space, with wet labs, prototype facilities, and coworking space. These facilities support over 60 tech-based start-ups in life science and other sectors.
- The university's student-focused DifferenceMaker program engages students from all academic disciplines in creating sustainable solutions via innovation and entrepreneurship (Figure 5.2). DifferenceMaker graduates have raised over $750,000 in start-up funding.
- The EforAll entrepreneurship accelerator in Lowell, with EParaTodos for Lawrence and Lynn, supports hundreds of early-stage entrepreneurs as they explore various retail, service, and tech-based start-up opportunities.
- Lowell Makes operates a member-governed 6,000 square-feet makerspace in downtown Lowell.

- The Lowell Development Finance Corporation, in partnership with the region's banks, established a one million dollar entrepreneurship loan fund, Launch in Lowell, that provides low-interest loans to start-ups that stay in Lowell.
- The city council designated an economic development zone known as the Hamilton Canal Innovation District.
- Middlesex Community College is integrating the university's student-focused entrepreneurship program, DifferenceMaker, into its own entrepreneurship curriculum.
- The city has partnered with the Coalition for a Better Acre, Community Teamwork, and the Working Cities Challenge to foster production businesses in the community among the city's various ethnic minorities.

These initiatives and collaborations are all relatively new, most initiated since 2012. The university did have existing academic programs in the business school that taught entrepreneurship; however, these programs had limited reach and focused primarily on students enrolled in the business degree program. The university's technology transfer office had met with some minor licensing success, most notably a stent technology licensed to Boston Scientific, but it was primarily focused on a push approach to technology

Figure 5.2. UMass Lowell's DifferenceMaker.

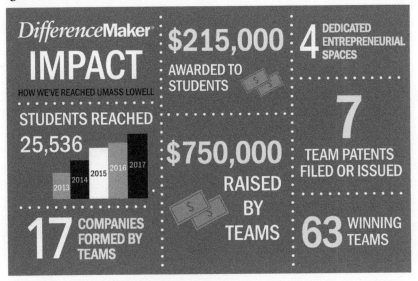

Note. The impact of UMass Lowell's DifferenceMaker program.

licensing, and engagement with the start-up community was limited. The university's medical device incubator, M2D2, was perhaps the strongest example of campus support for entrepreneurship, hosting 15 to 20 start-ups on campus pre-2012; however, student, faculty and community engagement in this effort was limited. It is reasonable to ask, *Why did an entrepreneurial ecosystem take root and blossom in the city of Lowell?* Let's examine this a bit more closely.

Roots and Catalysts in Lowell's Entrepreneurial Ecosystem

In examining the factors that contributed to the development of Lowell's entrepreneurial ecosystem, it is helpful to reconsider Isenberg's domains.

Conducive Culture

Lowell's ecosystem was not built with the benefit of an organized plan. Initially, there were limited financial and human resources to invest in this effort; however, there was a high degree of goodwill and trust. There was a sense that local university and community college students and the community would benefit if we could, first, increase the level of entrepreneurship support in the region, and second, attract entrepreneurs to the supports established. The university had graduated many engineering, science, business, and liberal arts students who had in fact become successful in their careers and as entrepreneurs. However, these individuals had done this as part of their professional career growth, and it was not the result of a targeted university emphasis on entrepreneurship programming. There was a sense that student/alumni engagement in entrepreneurship would increase if the university embraced entrepreneurship as a core value and then implemented programs that would support this commitment.

Beyond the university, city leaders understood the value of working together to promote economic and civic development. Following the decline of the textile industry and the economic downturn of the 1970s, city leaders did organize to help turn Lowell around. The Lowell Plan, a group of business and civic leaders who organized in 1975 to improve the historical and economic integrity of the city, helped chart a course of improvement for the city that resulted in the rehabilitation of dozens of downtown buildings, businesses, and neighborhoods (www.lowellplan.org).

Their efforts contributed to the founding of the country's first urban industrial national park, the creation of the 6,500-seat Tsongas Center, and a minor-league baseball park in the city. Consistent with an earlier reference to the "boot strap" nature of UMass Lowell students, the city itself understood how to confront adversity, brush off the dust of industrial decline, and move forward to implement new solutions and opportunities.

Supportive Policies and Leadership

The university's formal embrace of entrepreneurship emerged as part of the strategic planning process. In 2009, then-Chancellor Marty Meehan and Executive Vice Chancellor Jacquie Moloney (now UMass Lowell chancellor), initiated a formal strategic planning process for the next decade: UMass Lowell 2020. This process involved over 200 internal and external stakeholders and addressed a range of campus-related topics. Over the course of 18 months, 5 pillars emerged to guide the work of the campus. These were: Transformational Education, Global Engagement and Inclusive Community, Innovative Research and Entrepreneurship, Leverage Our Legacy & Our Place, and Entrepreneurial Stewardship in Higher Education (www.uml .edu/2020/Pillars-of-Excellence.aspx).

These pillars embraced the concepts of entrepreneurship, community engagement, corporate engagement, and experiential education. They established a priority and an emphasis on teaching and scholarship that supported the university's commitment to and engagement with the greater community. They also created internal grant and award programs that recognized and supported student, faculty, and staff projects that helped further the goals associated with each of the five pillars. The creation of an associate vice chancellor for entrepreneurship and economic development underscored the administration's commitment to entrepreneurship and established an office that would champion and coordinate emerging entrepreneurial initiatives. In other words, campus leadership backed pillar-related initiatives with funding and recognition.

About the same time, UMass Lowell engaged in its 2020 strategic planning process, another entrepreneurial leader stepped onto the Lowell stage. Gururaj "Desh" Deshpande, an entrepreneur, a founder of several highly successful telecom companies, and a resident of nearby Andover, Massachusetts, brought a new focus on entrepreneurship to Lowell. The Deshpande Foundation, supported by Desh and his wife Jaishree, committed $5 million to the establishment of the Merrimack Valley Sandbox, an entrepreneurial accelerator program that would specifically support start-up companies among the citizens of Lowell, Lawrence, and the region. This announcement, and the opening of the Merrimack Valley Sandbox in 2011, caught the attention of city leaders, nonprofit organizations, and the region's higher education institutions.

The Sandbox launched a Campus Catalyst program, which offered seed funding (up to $500 per student team) and entrepreneurship coaching to students of the 4 campuses in the region (Merrimack College, Middlesex Community College, Northern Essex Community College, and UMass Lowell). It also operated a social entrepreneurship leadership program that engaged the emerging leaders from the region's nonprofit organizations in leadership skill development around specific projects. Combined, these initial efforts helped raise the profile of entrepreneurship in the greater Lowell region among many different types of organizations.

Deshpande, a serial entrepreneur, is also well known for his philanthropic work, which includes starting the Deshpande Center for Technological Innovation (DCTI) at MIT. Through the Deshpande Foundation, he provided seed money to start the center, which empowers researchers to bring innovative technologies from the lab to the market place in terms of breakthrough products and new companies. Since 2002, DCTI has funded more than 90 projects with over $11 million in grants. Deshpande was honored by NACCE in 2013 with a Lifetime Achievement Award. NACCE President & CEO Rebecca Corbin connected with Steve Tello at UMass Lowell and Raj Melville, executive director of the Deshpande Foundation, at the 2016 Deshpande Symposium in Lowell. This annual event brought together ecosystem partners with university faculty and leaders who focused on entrepreneurship best practices. The diverse group of attendees shared innovative strategies for entrepreneurship curriculum and university research commercialization. Soon after the symposium, a partnership was forged between NACCE and the Deshpande Symposium to encourage community colleges to engage with both organizations and to intentionally seek greater collaboration in the higher education continuum for mutual benefit.

Institutional and Infrastructure Supports

In addition to leadership and culture, entrepreneurs need infrastructure and resource networks; they need spaces to meet, to gather and to build their ventures. While we all have heard the stories of inventors tinkering in garages until they raise their first venture round, the development of an entrepreneurial ecosystem requires more communal and engaged spaces. Lowell is fortunate in this regard, as a variety of spaces and programs have emerged to support the growth of our entrepreneurial ecosystem.

About the same time the Deshpande Foundation was launching the Merrimack Valley Sandbox (now called EforAll, https://eforall.org), the university developed a student-focused program called DifferenceMaker (www .uml.edu/differencemaker). DifferenceMaker launched in 2012 as an extracurricular effort that provided all UMass Lowell students an opportunity to create sustainable solutions to problems that matter to them and to our community. DifferenceMaker blends elements of design thinking and the business model canvas to raise awareness among students regarding the potential for entrepreneurship to help solve "big" problems and provide skills and resources to move ventures forward.

The program uses a range of in-class and out-of-class activities to engage and educate students, including pitch contests, idea hacks, hackathons, and workshops. The program also provides seed funding and resources to student start-ups. Since the first Idea Challenge in 2012, DifferenceMaker has awarded over $200,000 in funds directly to student teams. Seventeen companies have been formed (profit and nonprofit), and these companies have gone on to raise another $750,000. The program is now a core element of the UMass Lowell student experience.

The university, in partnership with the Commonwealth of Massachusetts, has also made a significant investment in technology-oriented start-up incubator space. In 2014, the university opened an additional 20,000 square-feet of incubator space in Lowell's Hamilton Canal Innovation District. The university expanded the successful M2D2 medical device incubator with an additional 10,000 square-feet of shared wet lab and BSL-2 biotech facility (www.uml.edu/m2d2) and also opened the Innovation Hub, a combination coworking, start-up, and prototype space for other types of tech start-ups (www.uml.edu/ihub).

These incubator spaces provide facilities along with access to university knowledge and research capabilities, and have attracted over 60 start-up companies in a variety of technology ventures to Lowell. In addition, the success of this model has attracted angel investment groups and major corporate venture companies to Lowell. The start-ups in M2D2 and the Innovation Hub have raised well over $100 million in private investment capital.

In addition to university spaces, Middlesex Community College, under the leadership of former President Carole Cowan and Vice President Phil Sisson, increased its commitment to developing entrepreneurial students (J. Hogan, personal communication, February 13, 2018). Middlesex Community College created an assistant dean for business, entrepreneurship, and legal studies and hired its first entrepreneurship program coordinator. Together, these faculty mentor students in the launch of their businesses, guide them in optimizing the Sandbox grants, embed active learning in the curriculum, and shepherd new curriculum to improve the teaching and learning of entrepreneurship.

As student interest in Sandbox grant proposals increased, it became apparent that students from all programs were interested in entrepreneurship. This led to the creation of Middlesex's Entrepreneurship Across the Curriculum initiative where faculty champions from all the academic divisions came together to learn about entrepreneurship and how to embed it in a variety of curriculums including science, graphic design, engineering, and the humanities.

More recently, Middlesex Community College partnered with the university to implement DifferenceMaker @ MCC (https://ideacentermcc .wordpress.com/difference-makermcc/). Working under the umbrella of the university's DifferenceMaker program has helped increase the involvement of Middlesex Community College students from across academic disciplines, while strengthening the presentations and business models of the student teams.

High-Quality Human Capital

In an entrepreneurial ecosystem, human capital is required in several different forms based on the stage of the venture. In the formative stage of a venture, an entrepreneur is needed, and depending on the type of venture, a lead researcher and perhaps a marketing and business lead are also needed. A small team is sufficient in the early days of a start-up when the concept is formative and resources are scarce.

As the venture evolves, resource needs change. The venture may need a production team, a regulatory lead, and more finance and marketing expertise. Beyond the start-up team, most new ventures also benefit from exposure to mentors and other entrepreneurs. Human capital comes in different forms with different types of expertise, and its value to the start-up is determined by the stage of start-up growth.

Lowell is fortunate in this regard. UMass Lowell and Middlesex Community College are investing in the development of the entrepreneur pipeline. Both institutions graduate a significant number of educated professionals with technical skills and know-how that complement the emerging industries in the region. Beyond Lowell, there are several other public and private community and state colleges that also contribute to this workforce, while the higher education cluster around Boston is only a 40-minute train ride away.

Beyond higher education, the microcomputer boom of the 1970s, the dot.com boom of the 1990s, and the current life science supercluster in the Boston-Cambridge area have blessed the region with a very high number of experienced, multi-venture entrepreneurs—individuals who either started or who have worked in several technology-related start-up ventures. This is important in regard to the need for human capital since these individuals can serve both as founders of and mentors to new ventures.

The Deshpande Foundation's EforAll program is an example of a start-up accelerator program that has successfully tapped into this network of entrepreneurial ex-pats. In addition to themed pitch contests, which attract and engage entrepreneurs, EforAll hosts two 12-week accelerator programs that match nascent entrepreneurs with successful, venture-experienced mentors. These mentors share important "lessons learned" with entrepreneurs and also serve as a gateway to additional needed resources, such as funding, scale production expertise, and marketing know-how. While employees work for a start-up, mentors work with the founder and the team, sharing knowledge and sharing resources. Both forms of human capital are critical to the growth and success of our entrepreneurial ecosystem.

Appropriate Financial Capital

Clearly one challenge to the success of any start-up venture is access to various types of capital. Start-ups require different types of capital at different stages of development. The type of company and product launched also impacts the type of capital required. A short-order cook who aspires to launch a food truck business may only require a short-term loan that supports the purchase of a truck and other equipment, while a medical device company based on emerging technologies may require research grants, angel investment, VC firm investment, and even corporate venture capital before the product is brought to the market. Again, Lowell has been fortunate in this regard; as the ecosystem has evolved, access to various types of capital has also evolved.

When the Merrimack Valley Sandbox launched its Campus Catalyst program in 2011 and offered student teams seed funding of up to $500, some people wondered what students could do with $500. However, the students' ideas were in a very early, formative stage, so $500 was helpful. They might buy supplies, use the funds to host customer meetings, or even buy simple software and low-cost computer prototype boards—the funds were helpful in testing ideas. Later, as student ideas progressed, teams could compete for additional funding from the Sandbox, the university's DifferenceMaker program, and even beyond at events like Boston's MassChallenge accelerator program. Prize funding is a key component of the ecosystem.

When the university launched the first M2D2 space in 2010, medical device start-ups in the incubator competed for $25,000 to $50,000 prototype development grants. These funds, provided by the Commonwealth's

John Adams Innovation Institute, would allow them to build a proto-type that in turn could attract higher levels of investment funds. These technology-based start-ups also competed for federally funded Small Business Innovation Research (SBIR) and Small Business Technology Transfer (STTR) grants, funds that could bring between $250,000 and $1 million to an early stage start-up company. These larger grant funds allow start-ups to retain equity while furthering product and market develop-ment. Grant funding is another key component in the ecosystem.

As investments in infrastructure and start-ups in Lowell grew, it cap-tured the attention of local banks, businesses, and realtors. Much like Lowell's earlier efforts to attract artists and the national park in an effort to revitalize the city, there was a growing sense of embracing this emerg-ing start-up culture in order to drive economic development in the region. Local banks and businesses became sponsors of EforAll events and university start-up spaces. They provided board guidance and access to philanthropic networks. Most recently, the Lowell Development Finance Corporation, in partnership with the region's banks, established a $1 million entrepre-neurship loan fund, Launch in Lowell, that provides low-interest loans to start-ups that stay in Lowell. The university manages Launch in Lowell application recommendations from the tech start-up sector, while EforAll manages application recommendations from the retail and community-focused start-up sector. These funds help keep start-ups in the Lowell ecosystem.

While the media tends to focus on IPOs and large venture capital invest-ments, these funds were really the last to come to Lowell. It took the launch of the university's second incubator facility in 2014 and aggressive, persis-tent outreach to various Boston-Cambridge angel network groups, to attract them to Lowell. With so many investment options in the Boston-Cambridge supercluster, investors asked, "Why travel to Lowell?" However, as EforAll expanded its mentor network (and program presence across the state) and the university's M2D2 and iHub incubators began to fill, angel groups began the commute to Lowell.

Today, over $100 million in private investment funds have been invested in life science and tech start-ups in Lowell. Groups such as Hub Angels, Boston Harbor Angels, Investors Collaborative, Golden Seeds, and Cherrystone Angels participate in pitch events and innovation nights in Lowell, hoping to find their next killer app or device. Complementing these angel funds are investments by larger, corporate partners. Johnson & Johnson Innovation Labs, Boston Scientific, Amgen, and other major cor-porations are investing in Lowell's start-ups and in the ecosystem, lending financial support as well as credibility to these efforts.

Venture-Friendly Markets

Invisible opportunity refers to the unexpected benefits that accumulate when you embark on a new and unknown path. When we started to explore entrepreneurship on the UMass Lowell campus, we had a very focused, disciplinary orientation. Entrepreneurship was a business-school discipline that could help turn our engineering and science innovations into tech start-ups. The university's early efforts focused on M2D2, the medical device incubator, and an undergraduate business major. However, over time, as new people, new initiatives, and new organizations entered the Lowell ecosystem, our experience, perspective, and opportunities changed in rewarding and unexpected ways.

First, we designed a richer campus program based on learning from others. By attending events at other campuses, we learned from their students and faculty, as well as from the Sandbox team. Second, we learned different methods of teaching entrepreneurship. While we were familiar with the technology commercialization and I-Corp models, we learned about the Ice House Entrepreneurship program and the Network for Teaching Entrepreneurship.

As a group, and with the support of the Deshpande Foundation, 30 of us traveled to Hubli, India, to attend a Development Dialogue conference and to tour the region. We learned about entrepreneurship at scale, developing a 10,000-student leadership cadre and turning them loose on the economic and social challenges of urban and rural India. We visited Akshaya Patra, an Indian nongovernmental organization (NGO) that feeds 1.6 million children per day across 12 states in India, and we learned about large-scale, entrepreneurial impact. In 2011, when I first volunteered to represent UMass Lowell on the Sandbox steering committee, I was expecting to teach, not to learn. These were all unexpected lessons.

But how do unexpected lessons turn into opportunities? Fast-forward five years. UMass Lowell has established an international partnership, the Global DifferenceMaker program, with KLE Technological University in Hubli, India—the same university that hosted the Development Dialogues in 2012. Our work with the Sandbox (and later EforAll) has helped deepen collaboration with Middlesex Community College, whose students now participate in our DifferenceMaker $50,000 Idea Challenge, and we share entrepreneurship curriculum (Figure 5.3).

Nonspec, our first campus-wide DifferenceMaker winning team (from 2013), is now working with partners in Hubli, India, to manufacture and sell its low-cost adjustable prosthetics at scale in India. A second DifferenceMaker

Figure 5.3. Nicholas Norcross (second from right) of Middlesex Community College and his partner Kevin Seery (second from left), of UMass Lowell, accept the Significant Social Impact award at the 2018 DifferenceMaker Idea Challenge.

winning team, invisaWear, continued on to EforAll, and joined Nonspec in the 2017 MassChallenge cohort, and has raised over $500,000 to build its personal safety device company (manufactured in Lowell).

The success of M2D2 and the iHub in Lowell has encouraged local developers to include next-phase start-up space in new buildings planned for the Hamilton Canal Innovation District, while existing mill owners are now converting loft space to lab space. Each June, the university hosts the Deshpande Symposium on Innovation & Entrepreneurship in Higher Education, a conference that attracts over 300 professionals and practitioners to Lowell to share best practices and lessons learned in building our respective entrepreneurial ecosystems.

These were all invisible opportunities in 2011, but now they are reality, serving to illustrate how we built the entrepreneurial ecosystem in Lowell, Massachusetts (Figure 5.4).

Takeaways

While Isenberg provides a helpful framework for examining the entrepreneurship ecosystem created in Lowell, there are several important lessons learned by the participants in this journey that are not captured neatly in his

Figure 5.4. Restored trolleys navigate the mill yards of Lowell as part of the city's rebirth as an urban national park.

framework. These lessons are based more on the personal experiences of the participants in this journey.

- *Raise your hand.* Step forward and volunteer to participate in new initiatives. This is particularly important for faculty and administrators who may already have full course loads and responsibilities, and who may not see or understand the long-term benefit. As administrators, it is important to give team members permission and time to explore initiatives that cross disciplinary and regional bounds.
- *Early collisions offer long-term benefits.* Initially, it was not clear how the university, Middlesex Community College, and other schools in the region would work together with the Merrimack Valley Sandbox to support student entrepreneurship efforts. Each campus hosted its own entrepreneurship events to varying degrees, and there was some concern over campus brand confusion and funding. These early collisions offered an opportunity to see how different schools and organizations recruited and supported students. They also led to the establishment of longer term relationships and partnerships.
- *Convening function is important.* Both the university and the Deshpande Foundation served as important convening functions; pulling together business, education, community, and civic

organizations around this emerging concept of entrepreneurship. The initial vision was not clear; however the foundation's commitment to Lowell helped to bring others to the table. Convening also provided a leveling effect, where voices from all organizations carried equal weight. Within our own organizations, we could make decisions about where our efforts and funds would be invested. As a broader group, we came to understand and respect the decisions and investments of others.

- *Open your doors.* Share your spaces and programs with partners and competitors. There are two lessons here. First, by opening your doors you can share and celebrate the work you have accomplished. This in turn allows others to learn from your experience. Second, by bringing competitors into your space, you build rapport and develop relationships. In Lowell, we have found that the different accelerator and makerspace programs in our city don't compete, but rather they help to build a bigger, regional identity as an innovative and entrepreneurial place.

- *Be open to other's models.* While each entrepreneurial ecosystem is context sensitive, you can learn important lessons by visiting other ecosystems and programs. In our journey, we visited the Deshpande Center for Social Entrepreneurship in Hubli, India; Skysong Incubator at Arizona State University; the American Underground in Durham, North Carolina; and numerous accelerator and start-up spaces in the Boston-Cambridge area. These visits helped us to understand how space, identity, programming, and scale are all important.

- *Don't overlook invisible opportunities.* Long-term opportunities are not always apparent during a first meeting or visit; it takes time to establish trust and common purpose. Be cautious about prejudging the long-term value a potential partner brings to the table. Allow sufficient time for you and your staff to establish a relationship and rapport with other ecosystem partners. As you build these foundations invisible opportunities will emerge.

References

Isenberg, Daniel. (2011). Introducing the entrepreneurship ecosystem: Four defining characteristics. *Forbes.* Available from https://www.forbes.com/sites/danisenberg/2011/05/25/introducing-the-entrepreneurship-ecosystem-four-defining-characteristics/#25db31785fe8; https://www.nps.gov/lowe/learn/photosmultimedia/decline.htm

Isenberg, Daniel. (2014, May 12). What an entrepreneurship ecosystem actually is. *Harvard Business Review.* Available from https://hbr.org/2014/05/what-an-entrepreneurial-ecosystem-actually-is

Meehan, M. (2017, July). *Report on annual indicators, university performance measurement system.* Available from https://www.umassp.edu/sites/umassp.edu/files/publications/2017%20Annual%20Indicators%20Report%2007212017%20F.pdf

Neighborhood Scout. (2017). *Lowell, MA demographic data.* Available from https://www.neighborhoodscout.com/ma/lowell/demographics

United States Census Bureau. (2015). *American community survey, 2015.* Available from https://www.census.gov/acs/www/data/data-tables-and-tools/data-profiles/2015/

6

THE ECOSYSTEM
THAT THRIVES

Deborah Hoover

*Kids carry the entrepreneurial torch naturally. They like the idea of running
their own business—the feeling of hope, independence and being in charge.
And they see entrepreneurship as a way to follow a dream.*

(Kauffman, 2005, p. 53)

A t a recent showcase for the Young Entrepreneur Market, a star attraction at Northeast Ohio farmers markets, preholiday shoppers were able to purchase a variety of enticing products ranging from wooden ornaments wrought from local hardwoods and fragrant soaps made from beer to pet beds crafted from sweaters. These innovative products are the result of a robust youth entrepreneurship ecosystem that encourages young people to be inventive and market their creations with the help of supportive mentors and educators. The evolution of this ecosystem is a story worth sharing with a goal of highlighting the organizations and pathways that bolster effectiveness. This chapter will chronicle the saga of building the youth, collegiate, and adult ecosystems in Northeast Ohio and the triumphs and challenges that have marked this journey over the last decade. The story will include the role of foundations, the continuum of K through 12 education programs, and the region's community colleges and universities working to promote entrepreneurship as fuel for economic revitalization.

Role of Philanthropy

In recent decades, Northeast Ohio has faced an array of struggles and setbacks precipitated by shifts in its industrial base, but these economic challenges have simultaneously inspired ingenuity and determination. To address complex challenges, philanthropy in Northeast Ohio has stepped up to advance the region's entrepreneurial ecosystem and its many tentacles.

Philanthropic leaders have been key players in strategizing and experimenting over more than a decade to reignite an entrepreneurial culture across the region. For example, foundations played a major role in establishing the Fund for Our Economic Future (FFEF), the groundbreaking philanthropic collaborative that has been bolstering the entrepreneurial ecosystem and economic competitiveness of Northeast Ohio since 2004. FFEF members believe that entrepreneurship is an important vehicle for transforming the Northeast Ohio region through the vibrancy of a thriving start-up community.

The Burton D. Morgan Foundation, founded in 1967, is the brainchild of Burton D. Morgan. Following a successful exit from one of his ventures, he started Morgan Foundation, which now pursues his vision of championing the entrepreneurial spirit. Decades ago, before entrepreneurship education was as prevalent as it is today, he recognized the need for aspiring entrepreneurs to gain the tools they need to be successful.

Longtime FFEF member Burton D. Morgan Foundation serves as an ecosystem builder connecting the people, ideas, and resources that contribute to a dynamic network of organizations focused on entrepreneurship and entrepreneurship education. The foundation approaches its work through the lens of venture philanthropy, employing strategic partnerships and catalytic grants to achieve its goals (Taylor, Strom, & Renz, 2014). In the relationships the foundation pursues, collaboration has become a critical element as a way to pool resources and amplify impact. The foundation supplements its grants with behind-the-scenes work to help grantees network, build strong programs, share results, and raise additional support. This hand-in-hand work with partners navigating the pitfalls together over time has nurtured an atmosphere of trust and shared mission. The foundation is an entrepreneurial enterprise, both influencing and adapting to the shifting entrepreneurial landscape in the region.

Entrepreneurial Pathways

Generating pathways that connect programs to the community and to each other has become an ecosystem mantra for Northeast Ohio. The Veale Foundation shares this passion and supports a key component of the Northeast Ohio youth entrepreneurship ecosystem through its ongoing sponsorship of the Veale Youth Entrepreneurship Forum, which is designed "to instill an entrepreneurial mindset in high school students . . . through a collaborative network of educators and business leaders [that] champion exceptional education and real-world experiences in entrepreneurship" (Veale Youth Entrepreneurship Forum, 2016). Veale Foundation has assembled a group of more than 20 high schools in the region with a goal of fostering a learning community and mentored opportunities for students to develop and articulate their entrepreneurial ideas through events and pitch competitions. These events draw students to college campuses where they are able learn about innovation and entrepreneurship at the university level.

Program sustainability is also of great importance to the Northeast Ohio funding community. A key factor in ecosystem evolution has been the steadfast, long-term commitment of regional leadership over more than a decade. This commitment is coupled with collaborative practices, strong metrics, research, and informed decision-making. Philanthropy has seeded many effective programs, but grant recipients must always address the need for future funding possibilities, including attracting other grantors and integrating programs into core budgets. Fortunately, entrepreneurship education in Northeast Ohio has achieved such a sufficiently high profile that some organizations are now able to hold major fundraising events to bolster entrepreneurship program budgets.

Entrepreneurial Ecosystem Experimentation

Northeast Ohio has transformed its vexing economic struggles into a platform for launching new approaches to entrepreneurship and entrepreneurship education. In the process, the region has evolved into a laboratory for ecosystem experimentation. Ecosystem partners over more than a decade have piloted a multitude of programs aimed at identifying best practices, creating a renewed culture of innovation, and engaging the larger community in fostering the entrepreneurial spirit. This broad-based approach is focused on designing initiatives and supporting programs that introduce grade-schoolers to entrepreneurial concepts, provide college students with mentored start-up experiences, and deliver just-in-time learning to adults navigating perplexing entrepreneurial journeys.

Over the last decade, philanthropy has played a pivotal role in spearheading development of a robust entrepreneurship ecosystem aimed at providing entrepreneurship education to young people. The work of Northeast Ohio's philanthropic community contributed substantially to the comment made in 2012 by Network for Teaching Entrepreneurship founder Steve Mariotti that Northeast Ohio has one of the strongest entrepreneurship education ecosystems in the world (Mariotti, 2012). Mariotti reflected on his own dedication to youth entrepreneurship in the following statement:

> To me it doesn't matter if these young people choose an entrepreneurial path to the future. The simple act of opening the door of entrepreneurial possibility in a young person's mind is what counts. The fundamental experience of coming up with a business idea and creating a business plan bundled with learning business skills and success-oriented attitudes can become a launching pad for a more hopeful, productive, and engaging life. It gives students ownership and control of their lives. (p. 68)

Mariotti's view on the multifaceted goals of entrepreneurship education coincides with the values of the field's most energetic proponents of the idea that for young people, entrepreneurship education can yield a variety of important side benefits by stoking curiosity, building confidence, enlivening core subjects, and enhancing problem-solving skills. The key is building the entrepreneurial mindset in students as a basic skill for navigating life and future career choices. In essence, entrepreneurship education teaches kids how to become tomorrow's dreamers and doers.

Community colleges are uniquely positioned to serve as leaders in transforming traditional vocational education opportunities to offer entrepreneurship as a viable career choice. By focusing on displaced workers, Lorain County Community College (LCCC) in Elyria, Ohio, "made the strategic decision to focus on building an entrepreneurship program and culture on its campus by offering experiential learning opportunities through a LaunchPad initiative that was recognized by Morgan Foundation with a grant of $3.2 million" (Corbin, 2015, p. 20). This focus on entrepreneurship was replicated in the southern part of Ohio through the work of Hocking College and Shawnee State University; both have joined the National Association for Community College Entrepreneurship's (NACCE) community of practice funded by the Appalachian Regional Commission (ARC).

Northeast Ohio offers entrepreneurship opportunities for young people through a variety of programs, including the region-wide adoption of the national Lemonade Day program, teaching grade-schoolers the fundamentals of business through the vehicle of the all-American lemonade stand. Lemonade Day is supported by entire communities that rally to provide sites for stands, loan boards, and most importantly, generate customers. The ecosystem serves as an important network that provides a wide variety of options for young people seeking an entrepreneurial experience. With many avenues to pursue from Junior Achievement and Camp Invention, to Entrepreneurial Engagement Ohio, there is no wrong door for entry into the region's abundant offerings.

Western Reserve Historical Society (WRHS) based in Cleveland, Ohio, provides another great example of adaptive use of the region's assets to help students develop the entrepreneurial mindset. Since 2013, Morgan Foundation has provided a series of multiyear grants for WRHS to institute a program in partnership with the Cleveland Metropolitan School District aimed at providing every 4th, 5th, and 6th grader in the system with entrepreneurship education opportunities. As keeper of Northeast Ohio's industrial heritage, WRHS relies on its rich collection of resources at the History Center and Hale Farm & Village to teach children about entrepreneurship from colonial times to the present. The lessons taught in each grade build upon the previous year and eventually lead to hands-on entrepreneurship opportunities in 7th grade. The program has expanded its capacity year after year and is currently serving more than 5,000 children each school year.

Once students are immersed in a program that piques their interest, well-recognized pathways guide the way for students to pursue more advanced and challenging opportunities. These pathways lead from grade school, to high school, and to college, as well as adult programs, and they encompass both curricular and cocurricular possibilities. While Northeast Ohio youth entrepreneurship champions have often shared the saga of building the ecosystem, its leadership is quick to point out that it is a vision rather than a model. The particular elements must grow from the unique chemistry and strengths of a region and are in a constant state of flux as the landscape shifts and circumstances change.

Intertwined Ecosystems

To truly change culture, a region must generate dialogue and build awareness of the power of entrepreneurship to transform an economy. Northeast Ohio has been dedicated to mapping its assets in order to better understand and share with the community the connections that exist among resources and programs. To that end, three entrepreneurial ecosystem diagrams—youth, collegiate, and adult—have provided a guiding light to aspiring entrepreneurs and their champions as they seek to navigate the start-up journey (Figure 6.1) (Burton D. Morgan Foundation, n.d.a.).

The Youth Entrepreneurship Backbone

The region's youth ecosystem has thrived because of the commitment of a backbone organization, Young Entrepreneur Institute (YEI), based at

Figure 6.1. Youth entrepreneurship ecosystem.

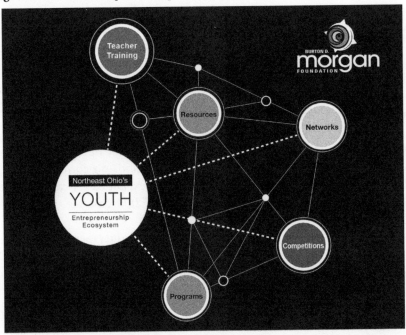

Teacher Training	Resources	Networks	Competitions
Enspire Conference	Entre-Ed	DECA Ohio	Bridging Engineering, Science and Technology (BEST) Medicine Engineering Fair
Network for Teaching Entrepreneurship	Foundation Center	Future Business Leaders of America	Cooltech Challenge
Real World Scholars	think[box]	Junior Achievement	Selling Bee
Wildfire Education Workshops	Western Reserve PBS	Network for Teaching Entrepreneurship	Teen Pitch Tank
Young Entrepreneur Institute	Young Entrepreneur Institute	Veale Youth Entrepreneurship Forum	ThinkBIG!
		Young Entrepreneur Institute	

Programs

Alpha Jump	Future Business Leaders of America*	Lemonade Day NEO	Western Reserve Historical Society
Consortium of African American Organization's Youth Innovation Forum	Greater Expectations Intercontinental Sacred Arts Society (GEISAS)	National Inventors Hall of Fame's Camp Invention	Veale Youth Entrepreneurship Forum*
Cuyahoga County Library's Entrepreneurship Summer Camp	Green Corps at Cleveland Botanical Gardens	Network for Teaching Entrepreneurship*	Young Entrepreneur Market
DECA Ohio*	Hudson Library & Historical Society	Ohio Business Week	Young Entrepreneurs Consortium
E CITY/Youth Opportunities Unlimited*	Invention League	Youngstown State University's Ohio Youth Entrepreneur Program	Young Innovators Society
Effective Leadership Academy	Junior Achievement*	One Hen (America Scores Cleveland)	
Entrepreneurial Engagement Ohio*	Leadership Ashtabula's ELI Program	Teen Enterprise	
Entrepreneurial Learning Initiative	Learning About Business*		

*This program has a competition component.

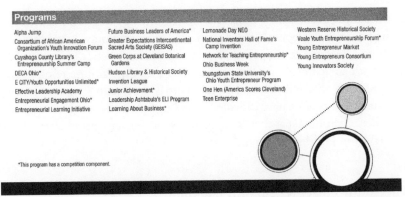

Note. The region's youth ecosystem thrives due to a strong partnership between the Young Entrepreneur Institute and the Morgan Foundation.

Source. Burton D. Morgan Foundation, Northeast Ohio's Youth Entrepreneurship Ecosystem, 2018.

University School, an independent K through 12 school for boys, founded in 1890. Morgan Foundation and YEI have been partnering on youth entrepreneurship since 2007, experimenting and pivoting throughout this decade of work together. The YEI staff coordinates regional programs such as Lemonade Day Northeast Ohio (NEO), Young Entrepreneur Market, Selling Bee, and Teen Pitch Tank. Greg Malkin, director of YEI, is the quintessential entrepreneurship education champion, working tirelessly, not only for University School students but also for students and teachers across the region to develop the best programs for their schools. Malkin offered the following insights on the importance of entrepreneurship education:

> Entrepreneurship education and real-world experiences position a young person for success whether they become an entrepreneur or not. Entrepreneurship teaches important life skills, including financial literacy and public speaking, but also stimulates a mindset that helps students to overcome adversity and take ownership of one's decisions. The entrepreneurial mindset strengthens the resolve of young people no matter what they do later in life. (Hoover, 2018)

Malkin combines his experiences as a technology entrepreneur, math teacher, and entrepreneurship advocate to consult with educators across Northeast Ohio on how they can inspire their students to think like entrepreneurs and lead the start-ups that will shape our future.

In the fall of 2015, Morgan Foundation and other sponsors worked with YEI to launch a dynamic regional entrepreneurship education conference (Enspire), now annually attracting hundreds of educators to learn from national experts in the field (Figure 6.2). The Enspire conference has become a cornerstone of the youth entrepreneurship ecosystem in Northeast Ohio. The conference offers a path to explore and understand different options that might fit the individual culture of a school and classroom. All teachers must figure out the best approach for their academic environment. In the fall of 2017, Enspire achieved record attendance when 375 educators attended the 2-day conference, absorbing critical tools to inspire their students to develop entrepreneurial mindsets.

Collegiate Entrepreneurship

Morgan Foundation's role of ecosystem builder also encompasses the ignition of the entrepreneurial spirit on college and university campuses. Morgan Foundation has partnered with two national foundations to support collegiate entrepreneurship programs on campuses in Northeast Ohio. A partnership

Figure 6.2. The Enspire conference.

Note. Entrepreneurship educators convened for Enspire 2017, an annual conference organized by the Young Entrepreneur Institute and Burton D. Morgan Foundation to help educators build the entrepreneurial mind set. Photo credit: Joseph W. Darwal.

with Ewing Marion Kauffman Foundation in 2007 resulted in a pilot program focused on cross-campus entrepreneurship programming on liberal arts campuses, known as the Northeast Ohio Collegiate Entrepreneurship Program (NEOCEP) (Thorp & Goldstein, 2010). Morgan and Kauffman Foundations contributed a total of $6.2 million to foster entrepreneurship on the campuses of the College of Wooster, Lake Erie College, Oberlin College, Hiram College, and Baldwin Wallace University. Now a decade later, the five campuses have thriving entrepreneurship curricular and experiential programs and growing numbers of students pursuing their entrepreneurial dreams (Figure 6.3) (Burton D. Morgan Foundation, n.d.a).

The NEOCEP program paved the way for the launch in 2012 of the experiential Blackstone LaunchPad programs (now NEOLaunchNET) on four Northeast Ohio campuses: Baldwin Wallace University, Kent State University, Case Western Reserve University, and Lorain County Community College. NEOLaunchNET programs emphasize the core educational aspects of the start-up experience as a growth opportunity for students. NACCE member Lorain County Community College LaunchNET also serves high school students on its Elyria, Ohio campus and at the new Lorain High School.

Figure 6.3. Collegiate Entrepreneurship Ecosystem.

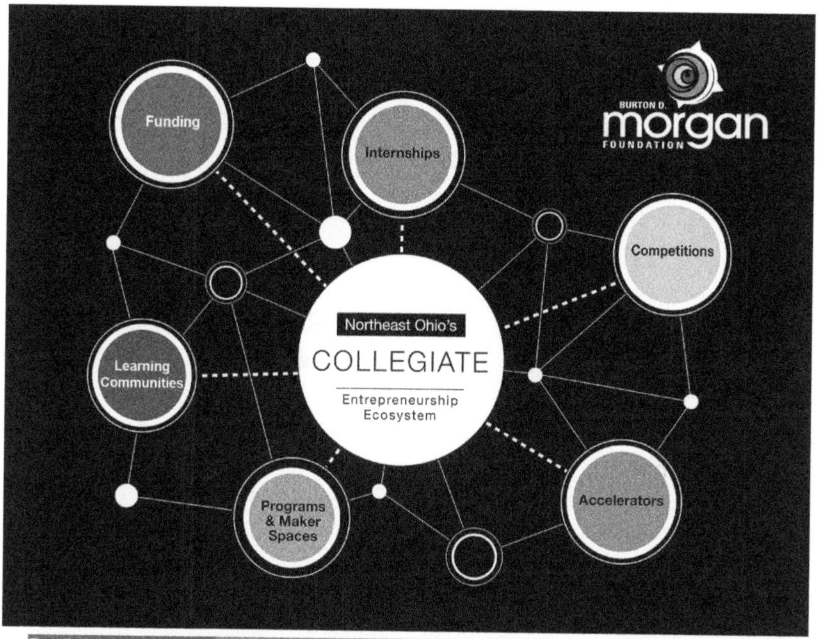

Funding
ArchAngels
Capital Access Fund of Greater Cleveland
Crowdfunding sites
Downtown Akron
 Partnership's Pop-Up Retail
ECDI
GLIDE
Hebrew Free Loan Association
Innovation Fund Northeast Ohio
JumpStart
Mahoning Valley Economic Development
 Corporation
National Development Council
Northeast Ohio Student Venture Fund
North Coast Angel Fund

Internships
BioEnterprise
Black Professionals Association
 Charitable Foundation's Career
 Connect
EDGE
Flashstarts
Innovation Fund Northeast Ohio
JumpStart
Northeast Ohio Student Venture Fund
Summer on the Cuyahoga
Venture for America
Youngstown Business Incubator

Competitions
Cleveland State University's Startup
 Vikes Weekend
COSE Business Pitch Competition
Flashstarts
FUEL at Bit Factory
Hudson Library & Historical Society's
 Pitch Night
ideaLabs
Kent State University's Fashion Tech
 Hackathon
LaunchTown
[M]Spire
Pitch U
SEA Change
SkyHack
StartupBus

Accelerators
Aviatra Accelerators
Bit Factory
Bounce
Braintree Business Development Center
Cleveland Culinary Launch Kitchen
Flashstarts
GLIDE
JumpStart's Burton D. Morgan
 Mentoring Program
LakeStart
LaunchHouse
REDIzone at NEOMED
Small Businesses Program
StartMart
The Incubator at MAGNET
Tri-C Goldman Sachs 10,000
Youngstown Business Incubator

Programs & Maker Spaces
Akron Makerspace
Akron-Summit County Public Library
 Entrepreneurship Center
NEOLaunchNET
Cleveland Culinary Launch Kitchen
Cleveland Public Library's TechCentral
 MakerSpace
Global Entrepreneurship Week

Hackathons/start-up weekends
Hudson Library & Historical Society's
 Morgan Entrepreneurship Center
Entrepreneurship Immersion Week
I-Corps Sites
Intellectual Property Venture Clinic,
 Case Western Reserve University
LCCC Fab Lab

Northeast Ohio Student Venture Fund
SCORE
Small Entrepreneur and Economic
 Development (SEED) Legal Clinic,
 The University of Akron
Spark Innnovation Studio KSU
Tech Belt Energy Innovation Center
think[box]

Learning Communities
Entrepreneurship Education Consortium
JumpStart Higher Education Collaboration
 Council
National Association for Community College
 Entrepreneurship (NACCE)
NEOLaunchNET
Northeast Ohio Student Venture Fund

JumpStart Higher Education Collaboration Council
Ashland University
Baldwin Wallace University
Bowling Green State University
Burton D. Morgan Foundation
Case Western Reserve University
Chagrin Falls High School
Cleveland Institute of Art
Cleveland State University
College of Wooster
Cuyahoga Community College
EDGE
Entrepreneurial Engagement Ohio

Hiram College
John Carroll University
JumpStart
Kent State University
Lake Erie College
Lakeland Community College
Lorain County Community College
Malone University
National Association for Community
 College Entrepreneurship
NEOMED
Northeast Ohio Council on Higher Education

Notre Dame College
Oberlin College
OARDC (OSU)
Stark State College
Team NEO
The University of Akron
University of Mount Union
Ursuline College
Walsh University
Youngstown State University

Note. Morgan Foundation's partnership with the Ewing Marion Kauffman Foundation resulted in a pilot program focused on cross-campus entrepreneurship programming on liberal arts college campuses.
Source. Burton D. Morgan Foundation, Northeast Ohio's Collegiate Entrepreneurship Ecosystem, 2018.

Collaborative relationships among college campuses in the region, beginning with the NEOCEP colleges and continuing with the award-winning Entrepreneurship Education Consortium, an 11-member collaborative of campuses that organizes opportunities for students to pitch their start-up ideas, connect students and faculty in synergistic ways, facilitating the cross-fertilization of ideas among the campuses.

JumpStart Higher Education Collaboration Council (JSHECC), jointly established in 2009 by JumpStart and Burton D. Morgan Foundation, connects campus entrepreneurship programs to the region's ecosystem. More than 20 institutions convene every other month for speakers, panels, and shared learning opportunities designed to enhance campus programming and student start-up experiences. JSHECC attracts a broad group of attendees representing colleges and universities, along with high school programs that intersect with the collegiate space, thereby enhancing a continuum of entrepreneurship education opportunities.

Northeast Ohio Student Venture Fund (NEOSVF) is a student-run, preseed capital fund that invests in Northeast Ohio start-ups with growth potential. With guidance, student participants perform the same activities that venture capitalists do, including generating deal flow, conducting due diligence, and negotiating terms. Currently, NEOSVF supports six chapters at Case Western Reserve University, the College of Wooster, the University of Akron, Kent State University, Notre Dame College, and Walsh University.

Pathways in Action: Youth to University

A major part of the ecosystem building effort over the last decade has focused on the creation of the pathways that guide students from one level of entrepreneurship to the next. Following are examples that shed light on connectivity among programs.

More than 1,200 high school students attended 1 of the 8 Entrepreneurial Engagement Ohio science, technology, engineering, and mathematics (STEM) forums held at Northeast Ohio colleges and universities in 2016. The participating institutions included Youngstown State University, Hiram College, Lorain County Community College, John Carroll University, Kent State University, Cleveland State University, and Ohio Agricultural Research & Development Center. At the forums, students heard a number of entrepreneurial STEM innovators discuss how their innovations help create the future. After interacting with the speakers, the students, assisted by college student mentors, were tasked to work in teams to develop a new product, service, or problem-solving innovation idea they later pitched to their peers. A venture adviser with LaunchNET Kent State University developed a high

Figure 6.4. Skyhack.

Note. College students brainstormed at Skyhack, the collegiate aviation hackathon, which was coordinated in 2017 with leadership from Kent State University's flight technology program and the campuswide LaunchNET program. Photo credit: Todd Biss Productions.

school entrepreneurship workshop designed to increase awareness of venture creation (Figure 6.4). Students learn about entrepreneurship via a *Jeopardy!*-style game, talking with a student entrepreneur, and working with a number of graphic organizers intended to assist with idea generation. With a case study problem in hand, the student teams circulate the Kent campus to solicit feedback from university students about potential solutions. While LaunchNET works primarily with college students, this high school program provides students with another pathway from the high school classroom to a college entrepreneurship program.

In the fall of 2016, the Veale Youth Entrepreneurship Forum convened high school students and educators from Cleveland-area schools for Thinkfest at John Carroll University (JCU). Conducted in collaboration with staff supporting JCU's entrepreneurship minor, the event led students through a series of exercises designed to help them think more creatively.

Pathways in Action: Collegiate to Adult

The idea of connecting university resources to the start-up community is not new. When the Ohio Board of Regents convened a Commercialization Task

Figure 6.5. Adult Entrepreneurship Ecosystem.

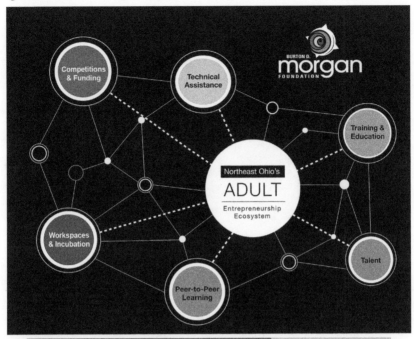

Workspaces & Incubation	Competitions & Funding	Technical Assistance
Akron Makerspace	ARCHAngels	BioEnterprise
Aviatra Accelerators	Capital Access Fund of Greater Cleveland	Commission on Economic Inclusion
Bit Factory	Cleveland 200	Hispanic Business Center
Bounce	ECDI	JumpStart's Burton D. Morgan Mentoring Program
Braintree Business Development Center	FUEL at Bit Factory	Launch League
Cleveland Culinary Launch Kitchen	Hebrew Free Loan Association	MAGNET/PRISM
Cleveland Public Library's TechCentral MakerSpace	Hudson Library & Historical Society's Pitch Night	The Presidents' Council Foundation
Downtown Akron Partnership's Pop-Up Retail	Innovation Fund of Northeast Ohio	SBDC
Flashstarts	JumpStart	SEED Clinic, The University of Akron
GLIDE	[M]Spire	Youngstown Neighborhood Development
Lakestart	Mahoning Valley Economic Development Corporation	Microenterprise Program
LaunchHouse	Medical Capital Innovation Competition	
LCCC Fab Lab	National Development Council	**Talent**
REDIzone at NEOMED	Northeast Ohio Student Venture Fund	ConxusNEO
StartMart	North Coast Angel Fund	Fund for Our Economic Future
TechBelt Energy Innovation Center	Seachange	TalentNEO
The Incubator at MAGNET	StartupBus	Team NEO
think[box]	Startup Scaleup	Venture for America
Youngstown Business Incubator		

Training & Education		Peer-to-Peer Learning
Akron-Summit County Public Library's Microbusiness Center	Hudson Library & Historical Society's Morgan Entrepreneurship Center	EDGE
Artist as an Entrepreneur Institute	Innovation Support Center	Entrepreneurs Organization
Better Future Facilitators	Presidents' Council Foundation's Excellence in Entrepreneurship	Launch League
Beyond Silicon Valley: Growing Entrepreneurship in Transitioning Economies, MOOC	Scalerator NEO	StartinCLE
Chinese Entrepreneur Association	SCORE	TechPint
Crafty Mart's Maker Series	Startup Scaleup	WIRE-Net
Cuyahoga County Public Library's ENCORE Entrepreneurs Workshop	Women's Network of Northeast Ohio's EMPOWER!	
Harrington Project	Youngstown Business Incubator's Women in Entrepreneurship	

Note. Higher education and industry are engaged in an increasing number of collaborations aimed at supporting regional economic development.
Source. Burton D. Morgan Foundation, Northeast Ohio's Adult Entrepreneurship Ecosystem, 2018.

Force in 2012–2013, members focused on energizing points of connection and articulated observations in the Sixth Report on the Condition of Higher Education in Ohio (Figure 6.5).

> **Collaborating With Industry**. Higher education and industry are engaged in numerous collaborations aimed at accelerating progress along the commercialization continuum and supporting regional economic development efforts.
>
> **Becoming More Market-Driven**. Universities and colleges are changing their philosophy and approach to both research and technology transfer on their campuses to reflect a much deeper understanding of industry needs and market potential. This is wonderful because market needs typically align to societal needs. Hence, as a society, we are using university commercialization to better address the quality of life of our citizens.
>
> **Promoting Entrepreneurship**. Task Force member institutions are engaging in a wide variety of creative activities to promote entrepreneurship among students, faculty, and community and regional partners and to help build a more robust commercialization pipeline in Ohio. (Ohio Higher Ed, 2018)

Northeast Ohio has achieved much in recent years to advance the ideals highlighted by the taskforce. Case Western Reserve University opened the Sears think[box] in 2016 as a center for innovation and entrepreneurship available to students, faculty, alumni, and members of the community to experiment, invent, and make prototypes. Located in a 7-story, 50,000-square-foot facility, this project is the largest open-access innovation center at any university in the world. The think[box] facility welcomes over 5,000 visitors each month.

Similarly, Lorain County Community College (LCCC) serves as a regional asset offering a vibrant campus ecosystem with multiple resources for its students and the community. LCCC is helping start-ups grow through the Innovation Fund and its Great Lakes Innovation and Development Enterprise (GLIDE) support services. Over the last decade, the Innovation Fund has awarded $12 million to start-ups across the region. LCCC is also contributing to the growth of clusters like additive manufacturing with the creation of a new associate's degree in applied science of digital fabrication technologies.

LCCC was an early adopter of the Fab Lab concept, a space open to students, faculty, staff, and the public featuring tools to conceptualize, design, develop, fabricate, and test product ideas.

LCCC's Campana Center for Ideation and Invention features state-of-the-art digital manufacturing labs with high-tech equipment for fabrication, automation, 3D printing, and more. It is surrounded by collaboration space and services to facilitate a full spectrum of product development–from initial ideation to prototyping, through assembly and packaging. The center offers hands-on education for students through college courses and K through 12 programs, while giving community inventors, entrepreneurs, and existing companies access to cutting-edge digital manufacturing capabilities.

The Campana Center deliberately connects the invention process to the marketplace through pop-up shops adjacent to the makerspace. This laboratory complements the start-up support services offered through LCCC NEOLaunchNET, an experiential entrepreneurship cocurricular program open to all students regardless of major. LCCC's NEOLaunchNET hosts weekly coffee gatherings of aspiring entrepreneurs through FEBEs (Fostering Entrepreneurship Business Education series), where business experts and experienced entrepreneurs share their stories.

Other examples of higher-education-to-business partnerships are described in the following three paragraphs.

EDGE is a nonprofit founded in 2005 that works to help mid-size companies grow through the exchange of knowledge. The EDGE Fellows Summer Intern Program provides 16 to 20 undergraduate and graduate students (fellows) with entrepreneurial internships at Northeast Ohio companies. Fellows are tasked with conducting market research on new business concepts and identifying the best ways to implement these ideas. In addition to being a valuable learning experience for fellows, participating companies have also benefitted greatly from the fellows' research and recommendations—approximately 50% of projects in the program's history led to further investment and/or revenue generation within 2 to 3 years of implementation.

BioEnterprise, a Cleveland-based accelerator for bioscience innovators, has worked with partners to create HIT in CLE, a health IT initiative. BioEnterprise is working with higher education partners, Case Western Reserve University, Cleveland State University, Cuyahoga Community College, John Carroll University, Kent State University, Northeast Ohio Medical University (NEOMED) and the University of Akron, along with high school partners in Cleveland, North Royalton, and Rocky River. BioEnterprise knows that talent is important to creating a vibrant bioscience cluster.

Founded in 1984, MAGNET (Manufacturing Advocacy and Growth Network) is an organization dedicated to helping manufacturers grow and compete in Northeast Ohio. To support and expand this work, MAGNET created the Partnership for Regional Innovation Services to Manufacturers (PRISM) to connect the expertise, technology, and equipment at higher education institutions more closely with growing manufacturing companies. Founding partners included Case Western Reserve University, the University of Akron, Cleveland State University, Lorain County Community College, and NASA. The program has expanded to include Kent State University, Cuyahoga Community College, Stark State College, Lakeland Community College, Ashland University, and Youngstown University.

Lesson Shared

As Northeast Ohio was beginning to experiment with the creation of its own youth, collegiate, and adult entrepreneurship ecosystems a decade ago, leaders in entrepreneurship education participated in a national learning community known as the Youth Entrepreneurship Strategy Group (YESG) under the umbrella of the Aspen Institute. During a series of summits that began in 2007, the members of YESG explored ways that entrepreneurship education could become a mainstream vehicle for preparing students to become the workforce and entrepreneurs of tomorrow. In recommending the widespread adoption of entrepreneurship education in America's schools, YESG observed the following:

> Entrepreneurship education helps instill an entrepreneurial mindset—a critical mix of success-oriented attitudes of initiative, intelligent risk-taking, collaboration, and opportunity recognition. This mindset is one of the real "secrets" of America's prosperity as it helps drive the creativity and innovation of our workers, our companies, and our entrepreneurs. This engine of innovation will be the primary driver of our future competitiveness. If you want America's young people to be fully prepared to succeed in the 21st century, nurturing an entrepreneurial mindset—via widespread use of youth entrepreneurship education programs - must become a core part of the American educational system. (Bell-Rose & Payzant, 2008, p. 27)

A decade later, America and Northeast Ohio have progressed significantly in their quest to embed entrepreneurship education in our schools. Based on its YESG participation and other experiences, Morgan Foundation prioritizes the sharing of knowledge we gain regionally, nationally, and internationally. In 2015, Morgan Foundation launched its Entrepreneurship Education Experiment (EEE), a research center focused on identifying and disseminating best practices in the field of entrepreneurship education.

Takeaways

Through the work of many bold partners, entrepreneurship has a stronger voice and a heightened role in Northeast Ohio. Our collective efforts over the last decade have generated a vibrant start-up culture and established our region as a place where entrepreneurs of all ages can grow their ventures within a dynamic entrepreneurial ecosystem. Key lessons collected over the last decade and the following basic tenets continue to guide our efforts:

- Educator training is essential to building the most effective programs.
- Philanthropy is critical to seeding ideas—collaborative partnerships among donors can work magic.
- Connectivity among programs builds the ecosystem, allows for shared learning, and benefits students as they discover pathways that work for them.
- The most vibrant programs grow from the essence and culture of the sponsoring organization.
- A wide array of programs in a region offers the most doors to students so they can find one that works best for their needs and interests.
- A long time horizon and patience are essential—it takes much longer than you would project to gain traction in creating an ecosystem.
- Community champions who will support the work over the long haul are key to sustainability and strong networks.
- Celebration of successes will build awareness and encourage others to build their entrepreneurial skills.

When we started this exploratory journey in Northeast Ohio more than a decade ago, entrepreneurship education existed on the fringes of mainstream education. This is no longer true. Entrepreneurship education has become an essential component of a twenty-first-century education, preparing students to enter a world in which they will be required to repeatedly reinvent themselves as technology and global forces generate rapid shifts in the economy and the workplace. Our goal as a region is to ensure that all students understand what it means to be driven by an entrepreneurial mindset that gives them agency to chart their own path and achieve their most ambitious dreams.

References

Bell-Rose, S., & Payzant, T. (2008). Foreword. *Youth entrepreneurship education in America: A policymakers action guide.* Washington, DC: The Aspen Institute.

Burton D. Morgan Foundation. (n.d.a.). *Home page*. Available from https://www.bdmorganfdn.org/

Burton D. Morgan Foundation. (n.d.b.). "What happens when the liberal arts and entrepreneurship meet?" *Intersections*. Available from https://www.bdmorganfdn.org/intersections

Corbin, R. (2015). *Generating revenue in New Jersey community colleges: An examination of entrepreneurship, philanthropy and workforce development practices* (Doctoral dissertation ProQuest No. 3732544). Wilmington University, Wilmington, Delaware.

Hoover, D. (2018, January 29). Entrepreneurial Foundation. *Small Business Magazine*. Available from http://www.sbnonline.com/article/entrepreneurial-foundation/

Kauffman Thoughtbook (2005). *The Possible Dream: Exposing Kids to the World of Entrepreneurship*. Kansas City, Missouri.

Mariotti, S. (2005) Opening the door of entrepreneurial possibility. *Kauffman thoughtbook* (pp. 66–70). Kansas City, MO: Ewing Marion Kauffman Foundation.

Ohio Higher Ed. (2018). *Report on the condition of higher education in Ohio*. Available from https://www.bdmorganfdn.org/intersections

Taylor, M., Strom, R., & Renz, D. (2014). Introduction. *Handbook of research on entrepreneur's engagement in philanthropy* (pp. 1–8). Kansas City, MO: Edward Elgar.

Thorp, H., & Goldstein, B. (2010). *Engineer of innovation: The entrepreneurial university in the twenty-first century*. Chapel Hill, NC: The University of North Carolina Press.

Veale Youth Entrepreneurship Forum. (2016). *Home page*. Accessed from https://vealeentrepreneurs.org/thinkbig/

7

CREATING AN ENTREPRENEURIAL ECOSYSTEM IN RURAL APPALACHIA

Charles Terrell and Joe Kapp

This chapter is about many things: perseverance and resiliency; small and rural communities and big cities; scarcity and leveraging available resources to make things happen. It is about challenges and opportunities and how one of the smallest community colleges in the United States, against seemingly insurmountable odds, rose to serve people in the community, regionally, across the state of West Virginia, and ultimately affected national public policy and entrepreneurial initiatives across the country.

Eastern is a small coeducational, state-supported, comprehensive, and technical college, established in 1999, and operating under the aegis of the West Virginia Council for Community and Technical College Education. Eastern serves a sparsely populated, rural six-county district in the Potomac Highlands that includes Grant, Hampshire, Hardy, Mineral, Pendleton, and Tucker counties, and it is more than twice the size of Rhode Island.

With a low population density and expansive geography, Eastern shares many of the same challenges that other rural communities across the country experience, including a lack of economic diversity. But from these challenges come a host of benefits that when leveraged, can be used to create opportunities.

A Sweet Spot

If you drive west for two and a half hours from Washington DC to Eastern's Moorefield campus, you will not encounter a single stoplight. It is a sharp contrast from the urban landscape of big buildings and commuter traffic congestion on DC's famed Capital Beltway. Eastern's main campus is located on a ridge overlooking the Potomac River valley and the Town of Moorefield, which has a population of 2,500 people.

The Potomac Highlands is one of the most beautiful areas in Appalachia with sweeping mountain vistas and an amalgamation of many small towns. Many of the region's families can trace their lineage back to a time when a young surveyor and future founding father named George Washington traveled the area. This population has largely descended from the earliest Scotch, Irish, and German settlers who moved to the area, living a hardscrabble life in the land that was once the frontier of a new nation.

In contrast, in the 1980s, urban professionals from Washington DC and its surrounding communities began discovering the region as a beautiful, affordable retreat in which to purchase or build second homes for weekend getaways. The natural resources, ample forests, running rivers, and idyllic setting with proximity to Washington DC, Virginia, and Maryland have made the region a popular destination for weekenders. A growing lesbian, gay, bisexual, and transgender (LGBT) population looking for outdoor adventures, mountain activities, and peaceful settings have also been drawn to the area.

As an institution, Eastern recognized its geographic significance. The recent development of a four-lane highway to Washington DC, coupled with broadband (fiber) Internet access by a local telecommunications cooperative, has enhanced the region's appeal.

However, the region has lacked a forum to bring together leaders to discuss challenges and more importantly, opportunities. With the impetus of a West Virginia law mandating that community colleges conduct regular regional meetings, Eastern believed it should lead the effort of serving as a convener through the establishment in 2012 of the Potomac Highlands District Consortium (PHDC), a network comprised initially of K through 12 and higher education representatives from the region. This consortium established an important foundation for creating an entrepreneurial ecosystem in the region.

In September of that same year, the PHDC hosted an Economic Development Summit for the first time, bringing together the K through 12 and college representatives with regional economic development directors and their colleagues. The summit revealed shared opportunities for the Potomac Highlands. Creating an ecosystem to support entrepreneurs and small businesses surfaced as a shared opportunity for Eastern's six-county district and emerged as a consortia priority. The summit led to a reengineering and expansion of the consortia invitation list to include:

- Economic directors
- Community development partners
- K through 12 representatives
- Eastern representatives
- Local entrepreneurs and businesses
- Local, state, and federal elected officials

As a result of the expansion, the group became known as the Potomac Highlands District Consortia and Economic Development (DCED) and became a statewide model for cross-county and regional collaboration. With the increased involvement and visibility, it also served as a tipping point in Eastern's role as a regional leader.

Entrepreneurship: What's Old Is New Again!

The reengineering of the DCED spurred a lot of interest. As word spread of the meetings, attendance climbed. With it came a recurring theme: entrepreneurship as a means of increasing economic diversification.

Entrepreneurship is nothing new for rural and farming communities. When one thinks about the original entrepreneurs, farmers and growers surely must be included at the top of any list. The mere innovation of planting a seed and waiting for it to grow meant that once-nomadic tribes were able to settle down and begin building stable communities that were a precursor to modern society. Today, the old adage, "necessity is the mother of invention," is particularly true in rural communities where access to resources, shopping, and even a qualified workforce could be miles away. Farmers who encountered issues on the farm—whether a broken piece of equipment or a cow stuck in a mud bank—had to be prepared to address these issues and others without the help of a nearby hardware store or veterinarian. However, somewhere along the way, farmers and rural communities—once stalwarts of entrepreneurship and innovation—lost their vision.

Attendees of the DCED continued to identify the importance of entrepreneurship as a means of reinvigorating the region and to help drive economic development. And so with the DCED input, Eastern had a new "mandate" to foster regional entrepreneurship and support small business development. It was with this mandate in mind that Eastern's president Charles Terrell signed National Association for Community College Entrepreneurship's (NACCE) *Presidents for Entrepreneurship Pledge* (*PFEP*) in 2012 to "ignite positive change across campus and in the classroom."

Another Tipping Point

That same year, on a brisk fall morning, as the leaves of the nearby George Washington Forest began to show their fall colors, it was during a casual lunch at the local Lost River General Store, where a chance encounter led to the introduction of Joe Kapp (chapter cocontributor) to Eastern's President Chuck Terrell (chapter cocontributor). Kapp shared his teaching experience, business background, and education background in economic development, and expressed an interest in teaching entrepreneurship the following semester upon relocating to the region. The weeks that followed led to meetings, phone calls, introductions to other entrepreneurs, and discussions on expanding Eastern's role in facilitating and supporting entrepreneurship, small business development, and creating an entrepreneurial ecosystem in the Potomac Highlands.

The Multiplier Effect: Making the Pitch

Kapp emerged as a student, a teacher, and a leader with a desire and a passion to understand the role of a community and technical college in developing an entrepreneurial ecosystem. The powerful synergy of an entrepreneur and a community college president eager to infuse an entrepreneurial mindset into the college's culture led to identifying new strategies for Eastern and the Potomac Highlands.

In 2013, Eastern attended the NACCE conference that included a pitch competition with the Coleman Foundation. The competition included a 5-minute presentation to pitch an idea for funding, followed by a 2-minute "elevator pitch" for finalists. Eastern presented a concept, under the auspices of Eastern's Foundation, to establish an Institute for Rural Entrepreneurship and Economic Development (IREED). Its mission was simple yet profound: to create, support, and sustain an innovation-based new economy in the Potomac Highlands of West Virginia and beyond. After competing against many other schools, Eastern won a $15,000 Coleman Foundation grant to establish IREED.

At the January 2013 American Association of Community College's (AACC) Workforce Development Institute conference, Eastern received an invitation to attend a meeting with the Kauffman Foundation. NACCE and AACC provided Kauffman with a list of 10 innovative community colleges known for supporting entrepreneurship education. The meeting led to Kauffman creating a group of 20 community colleges called the "Slingshot Network," which was designed to understand the role urban and rural community colleges might play in leading and supporting entrepreneurship within their regions. It was at the same time that Kauffman announced a $100,000

JOE KAPP: My first NACCE conference was a fascinating experience. After getting to know the attendees, I began to understand why NACCE was different. This motley crew of educators, administrators, and presidents were higher education's change agents. They were not your typical ivory tower PhDs. NACCE attendees were not merely content to simply study and publish findings. Rather, these professionals were actual tacticians—the ones willing to take risks, try new projects, help advance their institutions, and increase local and regional entrepreneurship in communities across the United States.

In addition to the expertise, NACCE members also had tangible assets from which would-be entrepreneurs could draw. From a wine incubator at Umpqua Community College in Oregon to a fabric and furniture incubator at Catawba Community College in North Carolina, across the United States there were community college assets and resources available to almost any kind of entrepreneur. In NACCE, I had just stumbled upon the largest, most tightly networked yet expansive entrepreneurial ecosystem in the world. Best of all, everyone I encountered was willing to share their technical information, curriculum secrets, their failures, and ultimately their successes. I quickly realized that the NACCE network had one of the biggest opportunities not only to change the role that community colleges play and the way they are viewed across the United States but also to substantially change the way systemic entrepreneurial ecosystem development is undertaken. In essence, NACCE had the ability to alter the role colleges play in making changes in higher education, and in doing so, at the same time, to create a process for the democratization of entrepreneurship. NACCE just needed the right leader with the vision, energy, and chutzpah to do so.

grant opportunity to establish an entrepreneur-in-residence program at 10 community colleges in 2014. In order to qualify for the funding, prospective colleges were required to provide a $100,000 matching grant.

Upon hearing what seemed like an insurmountable grant request, Terrell leaned over to Kapp, and said, "Joe, Eastern is out. We do not have $100,000 for a match. We won't be able to compete." Kapp paused, digesting Terrell's comment and then responded, "The problem isn't with the money. The problem is your attitude. The money is out there. We just need to find it!"

It was a bold and risky remark directed to a college president, but as Terrell now handily admits, it was a true statement. Sometimes the truth hurts, and Kapp's honest response served as a catalyst for change, influencing Terrell to fundamentally rethink his outlook and begin to adopt an entrepreneurial mindset. That leap to entrepreneurial thinking was a sharp contrast from the scarcity mentality that often plagues institutions dependent on state funding. Terrell resolved that Kapp was right, especially in light of shrinking appropriations; a different way of thinking was required.

In 2014, Eastern began developing relationships and outreach that ultimately led to Eastern's Foundation receiving a $150,000 grant from the Benedum Foundation and an additional $50,000 Advance Grant from West Virginia Community and Technical College System. Eastern was discovering the importance of crafting a "crazy quilt" and sharing its vision by engaging partners to create an innovation-based new economy (Sarasvathy, 2011). Telling Eastern's story, one of the smallest colleges in one of the most rural communities, became important. It began to generate interest, supporters, believers, and funders!

It's Alive!

With funding in hand, IREED could finally pay for Kapp's time and brought him on as its entrepreneur in residence with the objective of establishing a New Biz Launchpad (NBL), a business incubator with the fundamental mission to engage like-minded entrepreneurial leaders from the region. The site of the NBL was a small town of 300 people called Wardensville, which sits on the border of Virginia and West Virginia. Although small, Wardensville is strategically located so that more than 4,000 vehicles travel through the town as it serves as a natural gateway to West Virginia's beautiful scenery and outdoor activities.

The NBL is located in Hardy County, recognized as the largest agricultural area of West Virginia, largely based in the poultry industry. As Kapp met with people to discuss the new venture, he repeatedly encountered a common refrain. "According to town code, chickens are not permitted within the town limits," he would hear from local bankers and residents as he discussed the new project. Not coming from a farming background, it took Kapp some time to make the connection that every time he discussed a new incubator coming to town, the local community had a very different interpretation of what this meant. Chickens are raised in incubators, and incubators are not allowed within the town limits. This was a lesson in cultural competency. It was the first bit of resistance to the new venture, but it wouldn't be the last!

Trust and Relationships

It was with high expectations that Eastern opened the NBL in Wardensville, with services from our new entrepreneur in residence (Figure 7.1). While

Figure 7.1. Eastern's NBL.

Note. The Small Business Administration awarded Eastern $50,000 to help start the college's NBL.

many were supportive, this addition to a main street that had witnessed significant economic decline was surprisingly not warmly greeted by all of its citizens. During the initial launch, a smattering of placards appeared in town bemoaning the new economic development activities. Over the course of the next several months, what began as signs posted on a couple of buildings by a very small group of vocal detractors morphed into a larger campaign. A Facebook group surfaced that began a targeted campaign against the college and the new mayor, who was similarly trying to increase economic development in the tiny town.

On a regular basis, anonymous postings would go up on the Facebook page, which began deriding the Launchpad and Eastern. As the online assault became more consistent, the college maintained a position on nonengagement and nonresponse. College leaders expected some backlash. Any time change takes place, inertia and forces that have maintained the status quo are likely to resist, and this case was no different. It was the boldness and the inflammatory nature of the resistance that was most surprising.

However, realizing that the college was not going to engage, the online detractors continued to goad the college until the entrepreneur in residence was able to communicate the college's intentions and find creative approaches to dealing with the detractors. Eventually, he was able to disempower the opposition and move forward, in the process providing a valuable learning experience and inspiration for other colleges to "step into the fire" to help create beneficial changes.

In rural, suburban, and urban communities, there is the potential for resistance against innovative and creative thinking. At a tourism summit sponsored by Eastern, Todd Christenson, executive director of the Southwest Virginia Cultural Heritage Foundation, expressed a powerful sentiment, "Let the lone wolves hunt" (Christenson, 2017).

Community colleges are poised to facilitate community development initiatives that support the creation of entrepreneurial ecosystems. However, Eastern believes that its role is not to dictate creative interventions, but instead to lead inclusive discussions that potentially may not receive unanimous support. Sustaining an entrepreneurial ecosystem is dependent upon community engagement, collaboration, trust and positive working relationships. The best advice for a community college in rural communities is to always "take the high road" and not confront and/or challenge "the lone wolves."

As word of the college's endeavors spread, so too did the number of people seeking advice. Cautious at first, local residents began to reach out to the NBL as they began to realize its actual mission. It began with a voicemail from a local chicken farmer. "I have tried to develop a new product from chicken manure and I have exhausted every avenue. I would like to come in and meet with you," the caller stated.

Shortly thereafter, a diminutive man in a ball cap and jeans was sitting in the office of the NBL. Josh Frye, a local chicken farmer whose family stretches back for generations, began to share his story. He had developed a proprietary process for the conversion of chicken manure into a beneficial soil amendment called biochar. In addition to adding nutrients to soils and sequestering carbon, chicken litter biochar had the ability to attract heavy metals like mercury and lead. As a result, it could also potentially be used in remediation efforts of wastewater runoff. As the Eastern team delved into Frye's claims, the team began to realize that in addition to helping him launch his business, the college could be significantly involved in the development of entirely new industries around waste, waste management, and remediation.

The NBL team, now with the addition of a new executive director, Tina Metzer, began to focus time, effort, and resources in helping to expand Frye's business and potentially launch a new industry. This led to obtaining initial grant funding of $5,000 for Frye and the creation of Eastern's Biochar and Waste Initiative. In July 2017, with the help of grant funding to pay for speakers, Eastern launched the Biochar and Waste Summit. Word of this initiative and summit spread, bringing together over 60 in-person attendees as well as online attendees from as far away as Tanzania.

Since its start, the initiative has attracted quite a bit of unexpected interest and buzz, the culmination of which was a January 2018 *Washington Post* article, appearing in the Sunday magazine about the college's relationship with Frye and Eastern's journey to becoming one of the nation's most entrepreneurial

JOE KAPP: After working with Eastern and attending NACCE's annual conferences, I realized that the NACCE network offered a unique opportunity for funders and corporate interests to scale their impact in entrepreneurship, particularly related to hard-to-reach communities in both rural and urban settings.

In 2015, NACCE transitioned its leadership, and Rebecca Corbin became the new president and CEO. With this change came the opportunity to help identify the entrepreneurial activities at Eastern and find ways to scale them. In Eastern, Corbin saw a college that against all odds was embodying the heart and mission of her vision for the important role that community colleges could fill. In addition to focusing on some of the more traditional roles that community colleges play, such as two-year academic programs and workforce development, Corbin recognized that Eastern was a potential role model for other colleges: despite the challenges the college faced, it employed an entrepreneurial mindset to effectuate beneficial changes in a community, even with the most limited of resources.

Corbin understood the specific challenges that college presidents, faculty and staff, students, and colleges face. Just as importantly, she possessed the ability to effectively communicate and translate those challenges into ways that funders and foundations could support mission-critical programs and impactful work.

Nowhere did those qualities play out more prominently than during a visit to the White House during the Obama administration. Through relationships I had forged in my work as the cofounder of the nonprofit, LGBT Technology Partnership, I coordinated a meeting with the White House Office of Science and Technology Policy. During that meeting, I had the opportunity to see Corbin in action. In explaining the mission of NACCE and helping to craft some key deliverables from the White House staff, Corbin was able to drive conversations that would help execute the mission of NACCE member colleges. As a result of her efforts, shortly thereafter, we were invited back to the White House for an event with President Obama and the launch of a day of innovation and entrepreneurship.

Since that visit, NACCE's results speak for themselves: more partnerships, increased membership numbers, and greater funding opportunities for NACCE members and the execution of its mission.

colleges (Miller, 2018). Investors are now actively working with Frye to potentially invest in his business, and the college is now collaborating on grant funding to increase the scale and scope of this initiative.

The NACCE network offers a unique opportunity. The ability to work across an array of partners, organizations, institutions, and people to imbue a broad consensus of collaboration is critical for propelling ecosystems and prospective partners forward.

Entrepreneurship is not always about making money. Social entrepreneurship can have beneficial societal impacts without being profit-driven. However, not being profit-driven still means that organizations need to find sustainable business models to help fund ongoing concerns. Unfortunately, many nonprofits, educational institutions, and foundations focus solely on mission to the exclusion of a larger vision of sustainable funding streams.

Many nonprofits, educational institutions, and foundations have assets that are often underused. Used effectively, these assets could have helped to increase funding development opportunities or create sustainable models. By applying the principles outlined at NACCE annual conferences, Kapp founded a new nonprofit, the National Center for Resource Development (NCRD; n.d.). NCRD was formed to help mission-driven organizations derive greater value from existing assets or help build new ones to increase impact and organizational effectiveness.

Next Steps

Eastern has proudly stepped into its new role, serving as a beneficial agitator for economic diversity and entrepreneurial change by engaging partners interested in creating an entrepreneurial ecosystem. Although it wasn't always welcomed with open arms, Eastern's work continued to expand to include a broad host of partners and representatives. Since beginning the journey, the college has achieved a number of accomplishments, some of which were expected, and many of which would have been unknowable at the genesis of Eastern's work in entrepreneurship.

To support region-wide initiatives for creating an innovation-based creative economy, Eastern established new sector-base groups, including the following:

- Agriculture Action Council
- Arts and Tourism Council
- Allied Health
- Advanced Manufacturing, Technology Council
- K12/Career Technology Centers/Higher Education Committee

Each of the committees identified goals to support region-wide initiatives for creating an innovation-based creative economy. The results achieved since March 2016 are impressive. These new sector-base groups have launched a number of new regional initiatives, including the following:

- The Manufacturing Committee inspired Eastern to establish a partnership with Allegheny College in Maryland and Dabney S. Lancaster Community College in Virginia to collaborate on a joint request for proposal for a Department of Labor (DOL) America's Promise grant. The three rural community colleges are located in Appalachia and are connected by U.S. RT 220. America's Promise (AP 220) was awarded $3.6 million in January 2017 by DOL. This tristate grant is designed to grow regional partnerships among workforce agencies, education and training providers, and employers. By creating tuition-free pathways in health care and advanced manufacturing, participants are given opportunities to upskill and/or reskill to obtain competitively waged jobs.
- In 2015, the NBL and the Robert C. Byrd Institute for Manufacturing organized the first West Virginia Agriculture Innovation Showcase (Figure 7.2). This event has spurred numerous other activities, including a statewide infusion of entrepreneurship pedagogy in the state's high school curriculum and an expansion of the showcase across the state in subsequent years.

Arts and tourism are leading an effort to create a regional marketing brand for eight counties located in the Potomac Highlands of West Virginia. A Creative Economy Regional Tourism Summit in August 2017, organized through Eastern's IREED, introduced a regional tourism strategy to regional chambers of commerce, convention and visitor bureaus, community leaders and small businesses (Christenson, 2017).

Creating and sustaining an entrepreneurial ecosystem and innovative economy cannot be achieved by a single organization or community. Successful regional initiatives require talented, dedicated, and motivated "boots on ground" people who believe in regional strategies, but possess the time and skills to carry out the communications, planning, and support for organizing and engaging partners from a large rural region.

As Eastern's activities grew, recognition also grew that other rural communities across the United States have faced similar issues in trying to initiate and launch entrepreneurial ecosystems. The proverbial crescendo of events that Eastern has orchestrated includes the launch of the inaugural National Rural Entrepreneurship Ecosystem Summit, which was launched

Figure 7.2. Agriculture Innovation Showcase.

Note. Students from Eastern's service area attended the annual Agriculture Innovation Showcase, which brought together hundreds of students, farmers, and growers to explore agricultural innovation and entrepreneurship.

in collaboration with the National Center for Resource Development, the Rural Community Assistance Partnership, and Eastern. Taking place in the heart of Eastern's service area, this three-day event brings together national partners to learn from each other about the challenges, but more importantly, the opportunities that rural communities have in entrepreneurial ecosystem development.

Takeaways

- Attitude influences success. Eastern is proud of the recognition it has attracted regionally and nationally as the "little college that can" (Tucker, 2018).
- The college's student population is less than 1,000, but size does not influence success. It is okay to be small, but you do not have to think small.

- Let the lone wolves hunt. Not everyone will accept and join the campfire and sing *Kumbaya*. Take the high road and enjoy the view with great partners!
- Create and support a culture of innovation. The president is the role model and cheerleader. The president needs to lead by example. The goal for a rural community college president is to achieve recognition as an entrepreneur.
- Success is not a linear path. Have a vision, but remain open-minded when new opportunities are revealed, as this will definitely happen. The Launchpad was created to serve as a traditional business incubator. It evolved into the region's incubator for creating and supporting entrepreneurial ecosystem development. Be prepared to take risks and pivot when things are not working out.
- Share. Community colleges share a common bond—a diverse mission with limited resources. We change the lives of students when they are provided affordable, accessible education. We can change communities through facilitating and leading initiatives for establishing and sustaining creative economies.
- Leave egos at the front door. The vision is to build an entrepreneurial ecosystem, to create economic diversity so our communities can be resilient and our students can grow. We will never get the credit that we deserve. Understand that it is not about credit, but about a journey to improve lives. The entrepreneurial mindset begins with an individual, but flourishes when adopted as a culture of a community.
- Engage locally, think broadly. Presidents and colleges need to engage local, state, and national entrepreneurs to seek advice and serve as cocreators for an entrepreneurial ecosystem. Presidents need to maintain an open mind and be prepared for constructive criticism from entrepreneurs on how to blend academic and entrepreneurial mindsets.
- Focus on what you have. Too often institutions and communities bemoan what they don't have. Regardless of where a community is located, they have assets that can be leveraged. Even if it is chicken poop.
- Be a giver. Share your talents, your skills, and your experience. It will come back to you in uncommon ways and at unexpected times.
- Keep showing up. Persistence, consistency, and grit matter. People are watching and waiting to join on to success. Walking away when times get tough is easy. Staying in and continuing to work, especially at the most challenging times, ensures opportunities for success.
- Be authentic and be your best you. It is easy to forget that this path is a journey and not a destination.

References

Christenson, T. (2017, August 23). Potomac Highlands Regional Tourism and Creative Economy Summit, Eastern West Virginia Community and Technical College, Moorefield, West Virginia.

Miller, J. (2018, January 18). A liberal entrepreneur set out to help West Virginians— and got a lesson in humility. *The Washington Post.* Available from https://www.washingtonpost.com/lifestyle/magazine/a-liberal-entrepreneur-set-out-to-help-west-virginians--and-got-a-lesson-in-humility/2018/01/17/f6b0f5ac-e40b-11e7-a65d-1ac0fd7f097e_story.html?noredirect=on&utm_term=

National Center for Resource Development (NCRD). (n.d.). *Home page.* Available from www.resourcedev.org

Sarasvathy, S. (2011). What makes entrepreneurs entrepreneurial. *Effectual Entrepreneurship.* Available from https://papers.ssrn.com/sol3/papers.cfm?abstract_id=909038

Tucker, S. (2018, May). *The little college that can.* Commencement Address, Eastern West Virginia Community and Technical College. Moorefield, West Virginia, May 12, 2018. Available from http://www.easternwv.edu/communications-and-marketing/news-and-events/dr-sarah-armstrong-tucker-speak-eastern-west-virginia

8

COMMUNITY COLLEGES AS ENTREPRENEURIAL CATALYSTS

Madeline M. Pumariega and Carrie Henderson

Founded on the belief that all Americans should have the opportunity to achieve their goals, the modern community college's roots can be traced back to the 1947 President's Commission on Higher Education. Expanding on the junior college tradition that emerged in the early twentieth century, the report articulated a need for far greater accessibility to education for the American people, including women, minorities, working adults, and veterans (Cohen & Brawer, 2008). The placement of community colleges in local communities expanded their mission beyond serving as an extension of high school or preparation for senior four-year institutions. By their very nature, community colleges, which are now accessible to every town and city, are bridges to employment, both locally and regionally. By providing technical training and partnering with business and industry, the modern community college is positioned to serve as an entrepreneurial catalyst (Nesbary, 2015).

> Being entrepreneurial is essentially about thinking and doing something that we have not done before, in order to achieve a desirable goal or outcome. It is about assessing a situation, designing alternatives, and choosing a new way—or perhaps a combination of ways—that we hope will lead us to something better. (De Carolis, 2014)

In the context of the modern community college, entrepreneurship can be viewed through two lenses: first, through external facing, whereby community colleges provide resources for individuals and communities; second, through internal facing, whereby community colleges are entrepreneurial in their approach to serving students and meeting community needs. In the first section of this chapter, we explore how community colleges serve as resources to communities by offering academic and workforce programs and providing access to services for entrepreneurs and business owners. We also identify the community college role in economic development and social entrepreneurship. In the second section, we discuss how modern community colleges must be entrepreneurial in their operational strategies as a result of increasing demands and declining public resources. In the third and final section, we discuss how community college leaders can create an agenda for entrepreneurship.

At a state system level, the Florida College System (FCS) emerges as an exemplar for entrepreneurial community colleges. The FCS is a network of 28 community colleges, colleges, and state colleges serving nearly 1 million Floridians. It is the primary point of access to higher education in Florida, enrolling returning adult students and approximately 65% of recent high school graduates. These institutions are committed to providing the highest quality education programs to meet Florida's growing workforce needs while ensuring affordability and accessibility (Hanna & Henderson, 2014).

The results of these efforts are undeniable; FCS institutions consistently rank among the top community colleges in the nation. To date, Florida boasts the most finalists—14 of 28 colleges—for the Aspen Prize in Community College Excellence, the Aspen Institute's recognition of high achievement and performance among the country's top 150 community colleges. Additionally, 11 of Florida's colleges ranked in CollegeChoice's "50 Best Community Colleges for 2016-17," and 11 were placed in the top 100 colleges in the nation for the number of associate degrees awarded to minority students (Division of Florida Colleges, 2018).

Each year, the chancellor of the FCS recognizes innovation and excellence through the Chancellor's Best Practices Awards. The awards offer an opportunity for colleges to promote exemplary initiatives to statewide and national audiences by sharing innovative practices or enhanced existing programs. *Best practices* are defined as strategies, activities, or approaches that have been shown through research and evaluation to be effective—many of these practices are entrepreneurial in nature. Best practices can be new or refined programs relevant to academic affairs, student affairs, workforce education, business, economic development, technology, innovation, and administration as it relates to providing access, affordability, achievement and articulation, and attainment (Division of Florida Colleges, 2018). Throughout the chapter, we share examples of entrepreneurship at FCS institutions to illustrate different approaches to implementation as well as shed light on best practices that could be adopted by other colleges looking to engage in entrepreneurship.

The Community College as a Resource for Individuals and Communities: Education and Job Training

At a fundamental level, the modern community college's purpose is to provide education and job training through academic and workforce programs and community education. A primary mission of community colleges is to provide associate degree instruction in general education designed for transfer.

College Credit Programs

In addition to the transferable general education degree, community colleges offer certificates and degrees targeted to areas of need for the local community. Many community colleges offer certificates and associate degrees specific to entrepreneurship, often situated in business schools. According to data collected from the Integrated Postsecondary Education Data System (2018), community colleges in the United States conferred more than 1,700 certificates or degrees in entrepreneurial and entrepreneurial studies in 2015–2016. The Classification of Instructional Programs (2010) identifies these as programs that prepare students to perform development, marketing, and management functions associated with owning and operating a business.

Some colleges are modifying their curriculum to encourage students to embrace the entrepreneurial mindset through the Ice House Entrepreneurship Program. Drawing on eight lessons from *Who Owns the Ice House? Eight Life Lessons from an Unlikely Entrepreneur* (Schoeniger & Taulbert, 2010), students will engage in entrepreneurial thinking and develop their creativity, critical thinking, effective problem-solving, communication, teamwork, and other entrepreneurial skills (Figure 8.1). While some colleges offer the Ice House Entrepreneurship Program as part of entrepreneurship programs, many colleges are adapting the lessons across all disciplines through general education courses, workforce development programs for their faculty and staff, student success courses, or first-year experience programs (Ice House Entrepreneurship Program, 2018).

Community Education

In addition to the more traditional program offerings, community colleges engage in a broad array of community education programs emphasizing entrepreneurship. Community education is specific to local needs and may include areas such as continuing education, community services, and contract training. Community colleges offer community services in the form of

Figure 8.1. *Who Owns the Ice House? Eight Life Lessons From an Unlikely Entrepreneur.*

Note. Schoeniger, G. G., & Taulbert, C. L. (2010). *Who owns the ice house? Eight lessons from an unlikely entrepreneur.* Cleveland, OH: Eli Press. Used with permission.

cooperative agreements and community-based education programs designed to meet specific needs. Contract training may also be used to develop skills targeting specific industries (Cohen & Brawer, 2008). According to Nesbary (2015), nearly all community colleges maintain some form of entrepreneurship education or training. These offerings include courses, degrees, certificates, seminars, and workshops.

Makerspaces

In addition to traditional instruction, many community colleges are creating extracurricular opportunities for student engagement around entrepreneurship through makerspaces. A relatively new phenomenon, makerspaces provide students, faculty, and staff—and, occasionally, the public—with collaborative spaces to learn, create, and invent. With a goal of promoting entrepreneurship, makerspaces offer tools, materials, equipment, and training for students across disciplines (Barrett et al., 2015). Community colleges see makerspaces as vehicles for learning by creating a "maker culture" whereby students are more prepared for careers in the twenty-first century. In 2016, the California Community College system invested $17 million to fund makerspaces with activities including embedding entrepreneurship into curriculum, mapping stakeholder and partner ecosystems, developing skills badges and micro-credentials, and preparing students with twenty-first-century skills and work-based learning (Pepper-Kittredge & DeVoe, 2016).

Small Business and Start-up Support

Many community colleges are playing a role in local economic development by creating formal structures for entrepreneurs through small business development centers (SBDCs), incubators, and institutes. Emerging in the 1980s following a congressional act, SBDCs were designed to help individuals who needed assistance in starting a business or, for those who already have a business, providing management assistance. Expanding on the concept of SBDCs, many community colleges are creating incubators to assist budding entrepreneurs in the creation of new businesses. Through incubators, start-ups have access to networking opportunities, business services, equipment, and relatively low rent rates. Some community colleges focus their efforts on incubating small businesses in the specific skills where the community college has expertise such as technology or health care (Jacobs, 2012), while others focus efforts on reaching specific populations of students.

For example, National Association for Community College Entrepreneurship (NACCE) member Hillsborough Community College (HCC) partnered with the nonprofit organization Veterans Florida, with support from the Florida Legislature, to offer free-of-charge training and mentoring to Florida resident veterans who are active duty or who have been honorably discharged. This program is delivered in three phases. The first phase is an eight-week online class to provide a business education foundation. The second phase is on-site training at HCC over a six-day period across three consecutive weekends covering topics such as value proposition, ideation and effectuation, and customer relationship and channels. The third phase consists of six months of ongoing consultation with an SBDC allocated from existing resources.

Ultimately, the goal of this effort is to equip servicemen and -women with the necessary knowledge and tools to be successful in the global marketplace (Benstead, 2016). Given high demand, enrollment in the Veterans Entrepreneurship Program has consistently outpaced capacity. Currently, there are 8 veteran-owned businesses in development, along with 30 community partners actively engaged as mentors, advisers, and sponsors (Division of Florida Colleges, 2018).

In 2018, Broward College took start-up support one step further by launching the Student Venture Fund, which is a joint effort by Broward College and its associate organizations. This venture fund is designed to arm Broward College students and graduates with capital to launch businesses. Founded by Broward College President J. David Armstrong Jr., the fund leverages community and business partnerships to make financial capital available to students through a pitch competition. In order to be eligible for first-, second-, or third-place prizes, applicants must demonstrate demand for the product and service that is based in Broward County. The ultimate goal is to help student entrepreneurs turn ideas into businesses that meet the community's needs (Lima, 2018).

Relatedly, the Broward College Startup Now Accelerator, a joint venture with CareerSource Broward, brings participants through a six-month program in four stages: a boot camp where students learn about key concepts of marketing, entrepreneurship, and finance; lean launchpad where students engage in a flipped classroom experience; experiential learning by engaging with customers, industry members, stakeholders, and team-based learning; and Startup+ where students write a business plan and actually launch their businesses. Upon completion, students can earn up to 12 college credits in the entrepreneurship certificate (Broward College, 2018).

Economic Development

Community colleges have long played a role in the local economy through their academic program offerings as well as business-specific courses and customized training for local employers. Also, historically, colleges provide employers with student workers and serve as a launchpad to local employers through placement services (Young, 1997). According to Shaffer and Wright (2010), the changing economy and changing employer needs have further necessitated higher education involvement as an economic development partner. As the economy has evolved from agriculture to manufacturing to high technology to innovation, even greater demand has been placed on higher education institutions. Gone are the days when incentive packages alone were used to invest in businesses; today, higher education involvement to create a skilled labor pool is a critical strategy for economic development (Shaffer & Wright, 2010).

To that end, colleges and universities are directly involved by advancing innovation directly through technology and ideas, pursuing strategies such as business incubation and training to help local companies thrive, improving quality of life, and creating an educated population through credit and non-credit training and education. By engaging with the business community through program advisory committee membership, governing boards, and fund-raising efforts, for example, community colleges are fostering recipro-cal relationships that spur economic development (Shaffer & Wright, 2010).

Recognizing the economic power of small businesses, Goldman Sachs's 10,000 Small Businesses program helps entrepreneurs create jobs and eco-nomic opportunity by providing access to education, capital, and business support services. This approach is designed to spur economic develop-ment by resourcing growth-oriented entrepreneurs. The partnership-driven model—which includes higher education institutions, business development organizations, lenders, and professional service firms—increases the resources available to small business owners.

Babson College, in Wellesley, Massachusetts, cited as offering the num-ber one undergraduate entrepreneurship program in the country, plays a key role in community college participation in 10,000 Small Businesses. The col-lege designs and develops curriculum, trains faculty and business advisory boards, and designs evaluation and key measurements of the work. Further, Babson College works with community colleges to deliver the 10,000 Small Businesses educational component that supports faculty training and tech-nical assistance to program partners to enhance the entrepreneurial ecosys-tem. As of 2018, educational sites including community college sites were available in Baltimore, Chicago, Cleveland, Dallas, Detroit, Houston, Long Beach, Los Angeles, Miami, New Orleans, New York City, Philadelphia, Rhode Island, and Salt Lake City (Babson College, 2018).

Social Entrepreneurship

Recognizing that problem-solving, opportunity recognition, self-motivation, and resilience should not be limited to the business field, many community colleges have created programs to teach their students social entrepreneur-ship. Surging in recent years, social entrepreneurship at community colleges aims to prepare students for the ever-changing workforce while arming them with the skills needed to affect change globally and locally. This approach goes beyond service-learning and civic engagement. Through a multidisciplinary approach involving programs, courses, service-learning, student organizations, and student projects, colleges are equipping students with entrepreneurial skills and mindsets to help them address relevant challenges in their local communities (Schulz, 2016).

An initiative of the largest network of social entrepreneurs across the globe, Ashoka University works with colleges and universities to break down barriers to institutional change and foster a campus-wide culture of social innovation. This goal is accomplished through a multitiered strategy that includes the Changemaker Campus designation that recognizes institutions that embed social innovation in their culture; cohort-based Commons through which institutions receive expert coaching to build social innovation education programs; and the Exchange, convening to bring key stakeholders from across the world together around issues related to social entrepreneurship (Ashoka, 2018).

Entrepreneurial Ecosystem Champion and Convener

According to the ESHIP Summit Playbook (2018), traditional approaches to economic development that rely on attracting and growing existing companies are limited in their longevity and impact. To truly make an impact, communities need to invest in entrepreneurs by fostering an entrepreneurial ecosystem. Thanks to their ability to quickly respond to business and community needs, adapt curriculum to remain relevant, and advance economic development, many community colleges have joined others, including mayors, entrepreneurs, economic developers, and philanthropists by becoming champions of the work. Some community colleges have gone a step further to serve as a convener of community-wide initiatives. "As a college undergirds and supports budding entrepreneurs, it supports all segments of its community by creating, nourishing, and cultivating an entrepreneurial ecosystem" (McKeon, 2013, p. 88). By serving as convener, community colleges, inviting all key constituents to the table for discussion, contribute to an environment that ensures entrepreneurs have the talent, information, and resources when they need it most.

Idea Center at Miami Dade College: A Case Study on Entrepreneurship

Miami Dade College's (MDC) Idea Center is a shining example of an entrepreneurial community college (Figures 8.2 and 8.3). Open to students and

Figure 8.2. Students collaborate at MDC's Idea Center.

Figure 8.3. A student uses a whiteboard to capture inputs at the Idea Center.

community members of all disciplines, the Idea Center at MDC offers cutting-edge entrepreneurship education, professional development, and experiential learning to develop entrepreneurial ideas. Through the center,

MDC and community members are equipped with the necessary tools to develop solutions to vexing challenges.

In addition to offering an associate degree program in business entrepreneurship, MDC offers a 12-week Innovation Lab program that immerses students in an array of experiences and technology to explore their creativity. Upon completion, students have polished their technology and creativity skills. Under the Lean Startup umbrella, the StartUp Challenge places entrepreneurs in a nine-week program through which they pitch their ideas, attend workshops, and receive mentoring. At the conclusion of the program, participants present their business concept and obtain feedback from experienced entrepreneur panelists and peers from experts in the field. Idea Center at MDC also offers training in information technology and web development as well as marketing and branding guidance for business owners. MDC is also a member of NACCE.

The Entrepreneurial Community College

Community colleges are becoming more entrepreneurial in their operational strategies. This entrepreneurism trend is partially in response to declining financial resources from traditional funding sources alongside increasing demands. The 1960s and 1970s marked dramatic growth for community colleges in the United States. Funding for community colleges was designed to increase access to those traditionally underrepresented in higher education. As such, financial resources were allocated using funding formulas tied directly to the number of students enrolled. Likewise, the cost to the student through tuition was minimized. Taking cues from the private sector, policy-makers sought to increase efficiency of community colleges in the 1980s (Dowd & Grant, 2007).

These efforts of financing colleges based on efficiencies paved the way for modifications to funding formulas based on quality, productivity, and accountability. The 1990s and 2000s saw incentive or performance models supplant the enrollment-based models. With the changing rhetoric around college funding, state appropriations declined, and colleges began to see more revenues from grants (state and federal) and market-based services. Nearly 60% of college foundations were established in the 1980s and 1990s to fund-raise on behalf of community colleges. Collectively, these changes led to colleges seeking multiple entrepreneurial revenues to make up for loss of state support (Dowd & Grant, 2007). Resource development emerged as a primary means of diversifying funding sources. One notable resource for community colleges was the Trade Adjustment Assistance (TAA) program to establish a Community College and Career Training (CCCT) initiative. Eligible community colleges used funds to expand and improve their ability to deliver education and career training programs; in many cases, the grant activities were entrepreneurial by design (Mikelson, Eyster, Durham, & Cohen, 2017).

> The best community colleges will be those that are the most flexible and adaptive. The focus of the entrepreneurial college is not merely on making money, but also making things happen and developing resources so that the college can meet the needs of students and community. (Rouche & Jones, 2005, p. v)

In the face of many challenges, community colleges have adopted new ways of thinking and acting. Flannigan, Greene, and Jones (2005) include a number of strategies in their definition of *entrepreneurship*: strategic alliances, business and industry training, programming, foundations, fund-raising and friend-raising, outsourcing, and legislative lobbying. For these strategies to be successful, they usually involve cost-sharing and profit-generating (Flannigan et al., 2005).

Strategic alliances with community, business, and industry often lead to participation on advisory committees, student internship programs, and other initiatives. Business and industry training outside of credit and continuing education programs can also be a source of revenue for colleges; since they are not subject to state funding, they must be self-sufficient and therefore competitively priced. Community colleges may vary their traditional programming to be entrepreneurial by redesigning course offerings and exploring alternative modalities, as well as being flexible with session lengths. College foundations can seek private donations and engage in fund-raising to bring in sources of revenue. In an effort to reduce costs, community colleges may choose to outsource services such as maintenance, information technology, bookstore, and cafeteria. Lastly, many entrepreneurial community colleges use lobbying efforts to identify state funding sources in support of key mission activities (Flannigan et al., 2005).

Takeaways

For community colleges to be truly entrepreneurial, they must be willing to embark on a transformative journey grounded in responsible risk-taking, problem-solving, and creative thinking. Leaders of entrepreneurial colleges are facilitators, collaborators, consensus makers, and incentive providers. Their role is to cultivate a spirit of entrepreneurship across all areas of the institution by recognizing that people, more so than process, drive change (Rouche & Jones, 2005). In this chapter, we identified strategies that community college leaders can consider when trying to promote entrepreneurship on their campuses and in their local communities. To create a spirit of entrepreneurship, community colleges should:

- Consider embedding principles of entrepreneurship across the curriculum. While entrepreneurship programs will continue to be relevant in many community colleges, key concepts of entrepreneurship are valuable to students in programs outside the business department. The Ice House Entrepreneurship Program is a good example of how to teach entrepreneurship using an interdisciplinary approach.
- Invest in makerspaces. Along the same lines of interdisciplinary approaches, makerspaces promote creativity and innovation for students from many disciplines and programs. Incorporating makerspaces into courses and extracurricular activities encourages student usage, thereby creating a "maker culture" across the campus.
- Offer support to small businesses and start-up businesses. There are many resources and frameworks available for how community colleges can offer training, guidance, and support to small business and new businesses in the start-up phase. SBDCs provide a source of potential funding. Colleges can also seek investments from community, business, and industry to support incubators and investor funds.
- Engage in economic development for your local community. Having a seat at the table is the first step in promoting economic development. For community colleges to do this work, they must be equipped to create a highly skilled labor force for the jobs that are in demand. Creating reciprocal arrangements can boost college efforts.
- Create a culture of social entrepreneurship and commit to developing entrepreneurial skills and mindset in students across multiple disciplines to help them address relevant challenges in their local communities. Community colleges should explore the resources of Ashoka University, which has been engaged in the space with community colleges for years.
- Cultivate an entrepreneurial ecosystem. Community colleges play a key role in providing a talent pipeline for business and industry. They are positioned to serve as a convener of multiple stakeholders as well as a collaborator to ensure entrepreneurs are equipped with the necessary resources.
- Embed entrepreneurship into the college's culture. Community colleges should foster a culture in support of entrepreneurship. Including it in the strategic plan or signing a pledge to take specific

entrepreneurial actions are strategies that demonstrate institutional commitment to entrepreneurship through responsible risk-taking, problem-solving, and creative thinking.

While not an exhaustive list, these strategies can serve as a starting point in the journey to promote entrepreneurship in community colleges. Looking forward, community college leaders must be prepared for further challenges, such as waning government support, enrollment declines, and greater calls for accountability in student success and completion. New, less familiar challenges will be determined in the future as globalization and technology continue to advance. But with these challenges come great opportunity. Community colleges with an entrepreneurial mindset will be most prepared to seize these opportunities and thrive in an environment of uncertainty and change.

References

Ashoka. (2018). *Ashoka U about.* Available from http://ashokau.org/

Babson College. (2018). *Stimulating small business growth: Progress report on Goldman Sachs 10,000 Small Businesses.* Available from http://www.goldmansachs.com/citizenship/10000-small-businesses/US/news-and-events/multi-media/10ksb-impact-report-2018.pdf

Barrett, T. W., Pizzico, M. C., Levy, B., Nagel, R. L., Linsey, J. S., Talley, K. G., . . . Newstetter, W. C. (2015, June 14–17). *A review of university maker spaces.* Paper presented at 122nd American Society for Engineering Education Annual Conference & Exposition, Seattle, WA. Available from https://www.asee.org/public/conferences/56/papers/13209/view

Benstead, J. (2016). HCC to offer free entrepreneurship program for veterans. *83 Degrees Media.* Available from http://www.83degreesmedia.com/innovationnews/vetshcc011916.aspx

Broward College. (2018). *J. David Armstrong, Jr. STUDENT VENTURE FUND.* Available from http://www.broward.edu/discover/pressreleases/Documents/StudentVentureFundFlyer.pdf

Classification of Instructional Programs. (2010). U.S. Department of Education, National Center for Education Statistics. Washington, DC: U.S. Government Printing Office. Available from https://nces.ed.gov/ipeds/cipcode/Default.aspx?y=55

Cohen, A. M., & Brawer, F. B. (2008). *The American community college.* San Francisco, CA: Jossey-Bass.

De Carolis, D. M. (2014, January). We are all entrepreneurs: It's a mindset, not a business model. *Forbes.* Available from https://www.forbes.com/sites/forbeswomanfiles/2014/01/09/we-are-all-entrepreneurs-its-a-mindset-not-a-business-model/#11f4db33d84f

Division of Florida Colleges. (2018). *Florida College System 2016-17 annual report.* Division of Florida Colleges: Tallahassee, FL.

Dowd, A. C., & Grant, J. L. (2007). Equity effects of entrepreneurial community college revenues. *Community College Journal of Research and Practice, 31,* 231–244.

ESHIP Summit Playbook. (2018). *The ESHIP Summit.* Available from https://www.kauffman.org/the-eship-summit/overview

Flannigan, S. L., Greene, T. G., & Jones, B. R. (2005). Setting the stage for action: Entrepreneurship at work. In J. E. Rouche & B. R. Jones (Eds.), *The entrepreneurial community college* (pp. 1–10). Washington DC: American Association of Community Colleges.

Hanna, R. & Henderson, C. (2014). The Florida College System. In Friedel, J. N., Killacky, J., Miller, E., & Katsinas, S. (Eds.), *Fifty State Systems of Community Colleges, Fourth Edition (Mission, Governance, Funding, and Accountability).* Johnson City, TN: The Overmountain Press.

Ice House Entrepreneurship Program. (2018). *Higher education. Entrepreneurial Learning Initiative.* Available from https://elimindset.com/entrepreneurship-programs/higher-education/

Integrated Postsecondary Education Data System. (2018). *Completions: Awards/degrees conferred by program (2010 CIP classification), award level, race/ethnicity, and gender—includes new race/ethnicity and award level categories.* Available from https://nces.ed.gov/ipeds/datacenter/InstitutionList.aspx

Jacobs, J. (2012). The essential role of community colleges. In J. E. Lane & D. B. Johnson (Eds.), *Universities and colleges and economic drivers: Measuring higher education's role in economic development* (pp. 191–204). Albany, NY: State University of New York.

Lima, D. (2018, February 28). Broward College creates student venture fund for entrepreneurs. *South Florida Business Journal.* Available from https://www.bizjournals.com/southflorida/news/2018/02/28/broward-college-creates-student-venture-fund.html

McKeon, T. K. (2013). A college's role in developing and supporting an entrepreneurial ecosystem. *Journal of Higher Education Outreach and Engagement, 17*(3), 85–89.

Mikelson, K. S., Eyster, L., Durham, C., & Cohen, E. (2017). *TAACCCT goals, design, and evaluation.* The Trade Adjustment Assistance Community College and Career Training Grant program brief 1. Urban Institute. Available from https://www.dol.gov/asp/evaluation/completed-studies/20170308-TAACCCT-Brief-1.pdf

Nesbary, D. (2015, March). The community college as entrepreneurial catalyst. *Perspectives: Community College Leadership for the 21st Century.* Grand Rapids, MI: Ferris State University.

Pepper-Kittredge, C., & DeVoe, P. A. (2016). *Creating a network of community colleges with makerspaces: California's CCC maker model.* Available from https://ccc-maker.com/wp-content/uploads/2016/11/Pepper-Kittredge-Carol-Network_of_Community_Colleges.pdf

Rouche, J. E., & Jones, B. R. (Eds.). (2005). *The entrepreneurial community college.* Washington DC: American Association of Community Colleges.

Schoeniger, G. G., & Taulbert, C. L. (2010). *Who owns the ice house? Eight lessons from an unlikely entrepreneur.* Cleveland, OH: Eli Press.

Shaffer, D. F., & Wright, D. J. (2010). *A new paradigm for economic development: How higher education institutions are working to revitalize their regional and state economies.* Albany, NY: Nelson A. Rockefeller Institute of Government.

Schulz, A. (2016, Summer). Transformative learning through social entrepreneurship at community colleges. *Diversity & Democracy, 19.* Available from https://www.aacu.org/diversitydemocracy/2016/summer/schulz

Young, J. W. (Spring, 1997). Community economic development through community colleges. *New Directions for Higher Education,* No. 97 (pp. 74–83). San Francisco, CA: Jossey-Bass Publishers.

9

THE POWER OF
COLLECTIVE ACTION

A Five-Year Journey

Van Ton-Quinlivan

I n this chapter, valuable takeaways will be shared for community college leaders on how to create an intrapreneurial ecosystem that promotes sustained innovation; leverage change management and leadership strategies to solve complex education and workforce challenges; and integrate operational and funding models that foster a culture of experimentation and collaboration resulting in scalable, regional solutions. These practices have resulted in elevating funding for career education at the California Community Colleges from $100 million to $900 million.

From Local to Regional Perspective

The question of how to innovate market-responsive programs that are relevant to industry from a local to a regional perspective is a natural challenge for community colleges given political environments, funding requirements, and accountability measures. However, while colleges often focus on their local service areas, what matters to business and industry are both regional economies and available labor pools.

A locally driven model can inhibit collaboration, foster competition, and make it difficult to scale innovations across regions. Competition for funding often obscures the opportunity to work together to meet the needs of students and industry in producing more and better offerings. Given these cultural realities, the Chancellor's Office strategies for building scalable innovations to meet regional needs were threefold: first, to demonstrate the relevancy of career technical education (CTE) at California Community Colleges in addressing market needs; second, to fill the middle-skills gap by providing one million workers with industry-valued credentials, certificates, and associates degrees to contribute to economic vibrancy; and third, to apply new business models that drive innovation from a siloed and local approach to one from a regional perspective aligned to industry needs.

Employer-Driven Business Models

The PowerPathway workforce development at Pacific Gas & Electric (PG&E) was an employer-driven business model that was used to guide California's threefold strategy. This particular model demonstrated the power of collaboration in helping underserved populations while recruiting a diverse pool of entry-level applicants for the employer. Recognized by the Obama administration as an industry best practice in workforce skill development, key elements of the model included innovation, intrapreneurship, and business ecosystems while developing public/private partnerships to solve complex workforce issues within a sector (PG&E Corporation, 2016).

PG&E collaborated with community colleges within a region to develop a tailored curriculum, and the initial student cohort (43 students) received employment offers ranging from $19 per hour to $29 per hour upon completion. The project was scaled throughout the region, and an additional 250 people completed the program. Fifty-five percent of the graduates were women or persons of color and 60% of graduates were placed in entry-level utility positions (Rubin, Lizardo, Jamdar, Washington, & Zeno, 2010). Community experimentation, innovation, and risk-taking (intrapreneurship) at the regional level ensured that the curricula designed, instruction offered, and credentials provided to workers were aligned to the needs of industry.

Building on the approach of PowerPathway, California Community Colleges created a new framework, Doing What MATTERS for Jobs and the Economy, that established community colleges as essential catalysts for expanding the state's workforce and closing the skills gap.

Regional Framework for Innovation

In 2012, the California Community College Chancellor's Office implemented Doing What MATTERS, a unifying framework that drives intrapreneurship and innovations-at-scale, leveraging the network of the 115 colleges and 72 districts while also preserving their autonomy to allow for organic innovation. Staffed with a venture capital model of intrapreneurs responsible for developing innovative workforce development solutions collectively, Doing What MATTERS clearly defines a strategy with key priorities, high-impact sectors, and regional infrastructure that together ensure a shared and continued focus on the educational pipeline and sustained value delivery to the community. Guided by four priorities (Figure 9.1), the unifying framework encourages community colleges to collaborate with employers, workers, and students and work together to grow California's regional economies.

To have the greatest impact on California's educational pipeline and economy, the Doing What MATTERS framework targets industry sectors that are essential to the state's economic growth. The amount of funding allocated to a given sector is correlated to the number of regions that select the sector as a priority area. Industry initiatives are coordinated by sector navigators (statewide industry experts) and deputy sector navigators (regional industry experts) who regionally align community college and workforce development resources to 10 industry sectors and occupational clusters. Doing What MATTERS created regional consortia to align to these regions, which are supported by a consortia chair and/or cochair.

Once the framework was firmly established and structurally embedded, the California Community Colleges Board of Governors took the next step to address the state's gap in one million mid-skill credentials needed over the next decade. In November 2014, the board set the table by commissioning the Task Force on Workforce, Job Creation, and a Strong Economy (which

Figure 9.1. Doing What MATTERS for Jobs and the Economy framework.

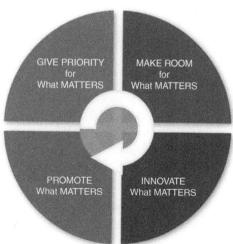

later became the Strong Workforce Task Force) to develop recommendations for closing the middle-skills gap.

Composed of knowledgeable leaders from across the community college system, the business community, labor, public agencies involved in workforce training, community-based organizations, K through 12, policy leaders, and other groups, the Strong Workforce Task Force would expand the table and broadly collaborate to develop appropriate recommendations. Over the course of 9 months, extensive input was gathered from more than 1,200 stakeholders from regional town hall and task force meetings to produce 25 recommendations across 7 broad areas as shown in Figure 9.2.

After an exhaustive process of data collection and analysis, a final report on the 25 recommendations was formally presented to the Board of Governors in November 2015, a full year after the Strong Task Force was commissioned. In June 2016, the California State Legislature approved the *Strong Workforce Program* to create "more and better" career education, and included a new annual recurring $200 million in funding. The funding is structured as a 60% Local Share allocation for each community college district and a 40% Regional Share determined by a regional consortium of colleges to focus on the state's economic regions.

Both the Local and Regional Share require local stakeholders to collaborate with industry and local workforce development boards. This program builds on existing regional partnerships formed in conjunction with the federal Workforce Innovation and Opportunity Act, state Adult Education Block Grant, and public school CTE programs. The Doing What MATTERS

Figure 9.2. Stakeholder task force recommendations.

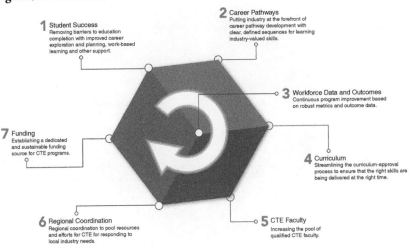

framework and the Strong Workforce Program work synergistically to ensure the organization as a whole can execute and meet the goals.

Alignment of Funding, Data, and Outcomes

Regional systems that involve a high degree of collaboration across multiple stakeholder groups require an alignment of funding and data to measure the right outcomes that move the collective needle, not just for a single organization. This was accomplished through the creation of LaunchBoard, a statewide data collection and visualization tool that drives positive student outcomes with actionable data on career education. Metrics include student outcomes such as long-term earnings of graduates, percentage of graduates employed in their field of study, and regional labor market information. The platform displays information in a visual format that provides insights into training the right number of students, equity gaps in student success, and student employment (California Community Colleges, 2017a). In addition, the platform readily catches red flags or areas of strength so that colleges can allocate resources as needed or locate strong programs at other campuses (Skvirsky, 2017).

According to Anthony P. Carnevale, research professor and director, McCourt School of Public Policy at Georgetown University's Center on Education and the Workforce, "The LaunchBoard makes the California Community College system the national leader in the development of data base tools for aligning student's career aspirations, curricula and labor market opportunities" (California Community Colleges, 2017a).

Transparency for Continuous Process Improvement

When the California State Legislature approved the Strong Workforce Program to create "more and better" career education in June 2016, California Community Colleges ensured that annual progress would be made visible with unprecedented transparency to practitioners via a dedicated section in LaunchBoard to enable practitioners to easily track and monitor performance and ensure that funding investments drive Strong Workforce Program student outcomes (completion, transfer, employment, earning, and skills gains) (California Community Colleges, 2017b). With this, the Strong Workforce Program put added focus on data-driven outcomes rather than activities and further fueled innovation and risk-taking (California Community Colleges, 2017a). Another level of data analysis tools, called NOVA, has launched to support regions in identification of potential strategies that braid funding streams to ensure students receive the resources they need to succeed.

Experimentation in Performance-Based Funding

Strong Workforce Program funding is divided among college consortia in 8 economic regions that receive 40% of the funds and community college districts that receive 60% of the funds. Eighty-three percent of Strong Workforce Program funding is based on the proportion of full-time equivalent students in career education programs, regional unemployment rates, and regional job openings. In addition, the legislation stipulates that one-sixth, or roughly 17% of the Strong Workforce Program funding, should be distributed using a positive-incentive funding model that aligns with the progress, completion, and employment measures established under the Workforce Innovation and Opportunity Act (California Community Colleges, 2017c).

The California Community Colleges Chancellor's Office convened the 17 Percent Committee, a group that included knowledgeable leaders from across the community college system and other experts to provide recommendations on incentive-based funding (IBF). To ensure fairness, the committee tested the model to ensure that first, it provided reasonable funding stability; second, it had positive funding outcomes when employment and earning outcomes were included; third, it had no inherent bias based on college or regional characteristics; and fourth, it did not pose any significant disadvantage to economically challenged students (California Community Colleges, 2017c).

The IBF model uses a point system whereby community colleges and regions receive additional funding for every career education student that makes progress within a program, earns a certificate or degree, transfers to a four-year institution, secures employment, or achieves positive earnings outcomes. Extra points are awarded for economically disadvantaged students. The Strong Workforce Program Positive Incentive Funding encourages local and regional workforce development strategies to develop "more and better" career education programs that advance and unlock social mobility for students (California Community Colleges, 2017c).

Celebrating Strong Workforce Stars

Using data to acknowledge, recognize, and celebrate innovation is an important success factor to reinforce efforts of early adopters and those that are meeting measures. The Strong Workforce Stars program fulfills this strategy and is an annual commendation for career education programs whose students show significant gains in factors important for advancing social mobility. Community colleges must meet one or more of the following criteria to be recognized as a Strong Workforce Star: student earnings increase by 50% or more; student attainment of 70% or more of the regional living wage; and/or 90% or more of students obtain employment in their given field of study.

Educational programs can earn more than one star depending on outcomes, and progress is tracked on a student success scorecard via the LaunchBoard. The state legislature is advised of the annual winners and an awards ceremony is held. Common program strengths of award winners include evidence of data-driven planning, outstanding career education faculty, a focus on being career driven, industry driven, and student centered, and intersegmental partnerships. In 2017, more than 100 career education programs delivered by 65 institutions in the California Community Colleges system earned a Strong Workforce Stars commendation (California Community Colleges, 2017e).

Innovations-at-Scale

Doing What MATTERS leverages a venture capital model of intrapreneurship that fosters collaborative, grassroots innovation, rather than a top-down approach. The system-wide infrastructure promotes local innovation by removing barriers and incentivizing community colleges to work together. Funding for program development requires at least 10 colleges to apply and work together in testing the concept, experimenting, and demonstrating evidence of success. Successful outcomes are shared, and the program is expanded to other community colleges to participate (Skvirsky, 2017). Following are four examples of program development at California Community Colleges that highlight this approach.

Experimentation in Badging: New World of Work Twenty-First Century Skills

The Economic and Workforce Development team at Feather River College in Quincy, California, was funded to conduct extensive research in 2012 to 2013 to identify the top 10 twenty-first-century skills needed in the new economy. With braided funding from adult education, CTE, and economic and workforce development sources, the team created 2 modules per skill (20 lessons) that they tested on over 200 Feather River College students. An Industry-Driven Regional Collaborative grant was awarded in 2015 to expand this pilot into a 10-college network tasked with working together to implement the curriculum. In 2016, the learning modules were expanded to include a digital badging platform in partnership with the Foundation for California Community Colleges to provide micro-credentials of skills (California Community Colleges, 2017f).

As of 2017, the New World of Work Twenty-First Century Skills Digital Badging program has expanded to more than 35 colleges and has earned accolades from the Mozilla Foundation, where it was named 1 of 2 promising practices nationally in higher education to develop and implement digital badges for soft skills (California Community Colleges, 2017a). The program partnered with the National Association for Community College Entrepreneurship (NACCE) to host a series of webinars for White House TechHire grantees to assist them in infusing twenty-first-century skills content into their training programs.

Experimentation With Learning Environments: California Community Colleges Maker

Launched in 2016 with $17 million in system funding, the California Community Colleges Maker initiative prepares students for the innovation economy via an aggressive 3-year statewide plan to integrate makerspaces into academic environments. In July 2017, the 24 selected colleges received funding to develop new curriculum, skills badges, and micro-certificates in alignment to workforce needs.

The California Community Colleges Maker initiative is the first large-scale higher education effort in the United States to launch a statewide network of STEM/STEAM (science, technology, engineering, art, and mathematics)-focused makerspaces that align New World of Works' twenty-first-century skills with STEM/STEAM research and supports work-based opportunities for students. Additionally, the project has created a national community of practice to distribute information and resources to ecosystem partners and stakeholders (California Community Colleges, 2017a).

Experimentation in Technology: From Here to Career Mobile App for Career Exploration

Developed by the Foundation for California Community Colleges, California Community Colleges Chancellor's Office, and Young Invincibles, Here to Career is a mobile application where users can view salary information and career opportunities in their area and find local community college programs near them to help achieve career goals. Funded by the W.K. Kellogg Foundation with a 2-year $375,000 grant, the first phase of program development focused on providing low-income Latino families and students in the Inland Empire with information, educational opportunities, and career paths that could increase their earning potential.

The initiative expanded, through funding from California Community Colleges, to other regions through an 18-month project called "The Work-Based Learning Planning and Tools Pilot." The pilot group comprises 34 colleges, including 6 individual colleges, 3 Strong Workforce Programs regional consortiums, and 1 community college district (California Community Colleges, n.d.a). Recent enhancements include regionally tailored information, improved usability, and a Spanish-language platform (California Community Colleges, n.d.a).

Experimentation in Apprenticeship: Building Capacity to Serve Non-Traditional Sectors

In 2016, California Community Colleges announced $15 million in new grants under the California Apprenticeship Initiative (CAI) to fund the expansion of apprenticeship programs statewide. One CAI awardee, San Diego Miramar College in San Diego, created a new apprenticeship called Innovative Apprenticeships for Life Sciences Industry (IALSI) across 9 apprenticeship career pathways. Rx Research Services, Inc. was the apprenticeship industry sponsor for IALSI and collaborated with 17 host companies in the region. Launched initially in Southern California, the long-term sustainability plan included expansion into Northern California for a total of at least 6 community colleges across the state that would maintain a pipeline of apprentices in the life sciences (Ton-Quinlivan, 2016).

Getting to the Tipping Point

Following are the five change-management strategies California Community Colleges used to create an ecosystem of innovators that drive large-scale change under Doing What MATTERS for Jobs and the Economy framework (Ton-Quinlivan, 2017):

1. **Engage with individuals who think beyond their own self-interests:** A critical success factor was identifying like-minded individuals who were able to think beyond their parochial interests in order to better serve students and their communities. This enabled teams to find common

ground with other stakeholders and work more collaboratively toward common goals versus in silos.

2. **Create a unifying framework for collective action:** The Doing What MATTERS for Jobs and the Economy framework focused on funding, metrics, and career education data on shared goals, making it easier for stakeholders to collaborate and lead employers to experience a more market-responsive community college system.

3. **Set the table, then expand:** As Doing What MATTERS for Jobs and the Economy continued to grow, California community colleges needed to build relationships and partnerships with the private and public sectors. By "growing the table," these stakeholders were empowered to participate and provide input continually. "Expanding the table" created ownership and accountability, and the motivation to undertake the large-scale change.

4. **Preparation matters:** As half of the Strong Workforce Task Force was directly outside of community colleges, relationships had to be forged to build trust and buy-in around recommendations. Creating a wide variety of communication mediums such as regional town hall conversations, coupled with transparent public vetting periods, allowed participants to be fully prepared for deep conversations that allowed for meaningful recommendations.

5. **Protect those willing to change:** When implementing new policies, the chancellor's office—the state agency overseeing the career education mission of the 115 community colleges—shielded early adopters by serving as the front line of defense. In doing so, those in the field were able to focus on collective measures and a mindset of innovation.

Optimizing the work efforts of those willing to innovate and drive change is a continual effort that is not easy but the results are worth it. Empowered to succeed, community colleges now reside within a cultural and operational structure to develop innovative programs and practices that drive student outcomes, increase social mobility, and contribute to economic resiliency.

Principles for Replication

With a state as large as California, effectively driving student outcomes requires an alignment of regional economies and industry needs. Focusing on priority industry sectors within this matrix is a means to target resources to produce the largest gains. Restructuring via a unifying framework enabled California Community Colleges to shift the state's focus from having workforce as an afterthought to becoming a state policy priority, which resulted in the annual budget for workforce development expanding from $100 million to $900 million.

Significant system change was necessary to refocus on delivering a skilled workforce that drives regional economies and advances social mobility. Looking back on what had the most impact throughout the course of this process, five best practices stand out and are described in the following section.

Takeaways

- Cultivate a collaborative ecosystem of intrapreneurs as a strategy to deliver system change. Leveraging the venture capital model for innovation, key talent was hired as intrapreneurs to solve problems on the ground as the colleges worked toward closing the middle-skill gap. By embedding a 360-degree feedback process to develop key talent, a high-performance culture of collaboration was created. Within this new ecosystem, model training programs began replicating within networks.
- Develop tools to "free the data." Help decision-makers see what matters. LaunchBoard was developed at the state level to support the field in capturing data and making informed decisions on metrics that matter. The level of transparency was unprecedented, as data were available to all practitioners, which empowered informed action and investment. Access to the right data that align with key objectives is a critical component to success.
- Innovations-at-scale. Solve problems that are bigger than one college, collectively. As the largest community college system in the nation, California Community Colleges needed to leverage its scale. Some issues were so big that they needed to be spread across multiple colleges to solve. This sort of experimentation allowed effective innovation and problem-solving to occur by harnessing the collective power of networks.
- Track the student metrics that count. In addition to the traditional student metrics of completion and transfer, California Community Colleges began tracking employment, earnings, and skills gains. These measures were incorporated into Strong Workforce Program Positive Incentives where a portion of a community college's funding is based on how well they contribute to student outcomes in their region.

- Acknowledge and reward success. California Community Colleges developed Strong Workforce Stars as a new, annual commendation for career education program where community colleges celebrate programs that show objective and significant gains for advancing student social mobility. With its focus on proving student success through data, Strong Workforce Stars reinforces its commitment to building a strong workforce for California.

By focusing on Doing What MATTERS we have reached a critical mass. This is the power of collective action. It's an accelerating factor that, when harnessed, creates a highly effective means to innovations resulting in social mobility and economic prosperity. As with any good journey, there is always another next step and always room for improvement. The next frontier is to parlay assets and learning from Doing What MATTERS into guided pathway design; to develop coordinated, regional business engagement ecosystems to maximize employer engagement; and to enhance students' educational experiences through technology platforms.

References

California Community Colleges. (2017a). *Economic and workforce development program annual report.* Available. from http://californiacommunitycolleges.cccco .edu/Portals/0/Reports/2017-EWD-Report-r2-ADA-Reduced.pdf

California Community Colleges. (2017b). *Strong workforce program incentive funding.* Available from http://doingwhatmatters.cccco.edu/portals/6/docs/sw/SWP %20Incentive%20Funding%20Model.pdf

California Community Colleges. (2017c, April 20). *Strong workforce program positive incentive funding model.* Available from http://extranet.cccco.edu/Portals/1/ ExecutiveOffice/Consultation/2017_agendas/April/Digest-Strong-Workforce-Program.pdf

California Community Colleges. (2017d, March 27). *Strong workforce program 17% incentive funding model analysis* (White Paper). Available from http:// doingwhatmatters.cccco.edu/portals/6/docs/sw/White%20Paper%204-Strong %20Workforce%20Program%2017%20Pecent%20Incentive%20Funding%20 Model%20Analysis.pdf

California Community Colleges, Chancellor's Office. (2017e, July 24). *Standouts in career education earn accolades as California's community colleges advance social and economic mobility* [Press release]. Available from http://www .californiacommunitycolleges.cccco.edu/Portals/0/DocDownloads/PressReleases /JUL2017/PR-STRONG-WORKFORCE-07-24-2017.pdf

California Community Colleges. (2017f). *New world of work 21st century skills for adult learners* (PowerPoint Slides). Available from http://aebg.cccco.edu/portals/1/docs/summit/21st%20Century%20Skills%20for%20Adult%20Education-%20Final%20RGill.pdf

California Community Colleges. (n.d.a). *About the work-based learning planning and tools pilot.* Available from https://www.careerexperiencesuite.org/pilot/

California Community Colleges. (n.d.b). *Here to career mobile app.* Available from https://foundationccc.org/What-We-Do/Workforce-Development/Here-to-Career-Mobile-App

PG&E Corporation. (2016). *Together, building a better California: Corporate responsibility and sustainability report 2016.* Available from http://www.pgecorp.com/corp_responsibility/reports/2016/PGE_CRSR_2016.pdf

Rubin, V., Lizardo, R., Jamdar, A., Washington, J., & Zeno, A. (2010). Pathways out of poverty for vulnerable Californians: Policies that prepare the workforce for middle-skill infrastructure jobs. *PolicyLink.* Available from https://www.policylink.org/sites/default/files/PATHWAYS_WEB.PDF

Skvirsky, S. (2017). *Charting new paths to the future in the California community colleges.* Available from http://www.iftf.org/fileadmin/user_upload/downloads/learning/IFTF_CCC_Charting_New_Paths_SR-1930_2.pdf

Ton-Quinlivan, V. (2016, 2nd Quarter). New grants fund innovative program for life sciences. *California Apprenticeship Council Newsletter.* Available from https://www.dir.ca.gov/CAC/ReportsPublications/CACNewsletter2ndQuarter2016.pdf

Ton-Quinlivan, Van. (2017). *Cross-sector collaboration: What the tipping point looks like.* Available from https://ssir.org/articles/entry/cross_sector_collaboration_what_the_tipping_point_looks_like

ENTREPRENEURIAL COMMUNITY COLLEGES— SUSTAINABILITY AND LESSONS FROM THE LEAGUE

Rufus Glasper

An Evolving Role

The evolution of entrepreneurial community colleges is a relatively new phenomenon, developed gradually over time. This development is in part based on an increasing need to supplement and, in some cases, supplant declining tuition and local, state, and federal funding. It is also driven by the fact that we have increasingly embraced our role as one of the major economic drivers in our communities. "Employers we meet with most often ask if we can get them the skilled workforce they need," noted John Rainone (personal communication, May 21, 2018), president of Dabney S. Lancaster Community College in Clifton Forge, Virginia. "We're now working as economic development experts. If not for community colleges, we'd have a shortage of EMTs, nurses, truck drivers, mechanics, welders and many other types of skilled workers."

According to Rainone:

Some might argue that by moving toward an entrepreneurial mindset and entrepreneurial activities, we are moving away from the foundation notion of community colleges, namely that higher education is a public benefit of and by itself. However, the move toward entrepreneurial thinking and action is not a move away from being a public benefit. In fact, this shift perhaps embraces that ideal more closely than ever before. As we work to prepare students for the twenty-first-century world of work and entrepreneurship, community colleges strengthen the American Dream. (J. Rainone, personal communication, May 21, 2018)

If small businesses are the lifeblood of America, then entrepreneurial community colleges are the lifeblood of the communities they serve and the states in which they reside. To envision this innovation as game-changing highlights its significance and potential impact on the world of work and the confluence of higher education institutions and businesses as linchpins vital to maintaining the bridge to the future. This bridge formed out of necessity and, in part, by the increasing practice of neoliberalism. *Neoliberalism* is defined as:

> A policy model of social studies and economics that transfers control of economic factors to the private sector from the public sector. It takes from the basic principles of neoclassical economics, suggesting that governments must limit subsidies, make reforms to tax law in order to expand the tax base, reduce deficit spending, limit protectionism, and open markets up to trade. (Investopedia, n.d.)

In our effort to survive and thrive as higher education institutions, we are moving toward operating certain areas of our institutions as small businesses, charting a new path for administrators, faculty, students, and colleges. However, to make such a significant shift, we must first embrace the concept of change management and all the elements involved that impact students, faculty, staff, and communities—specifically, businesses—in making this organizational change.

The entrepreneurial community college is helping to redefine "the larger purpose of higher education, beyond preparation for employment" (Zecher Sutton, 2016). Its creation and evolution over time provides a twenty-first-century framework featuring a new model for student and faculty engagement, new funding concepts, and stronger ties to institutional advancement and the world of business. Through its lens, we are able to see the disconnects and silos developed and maintained by previous institutional leaders and management in an attempt to fit into traditional operating structures. This take-charge approach to management of our own destiny is welcomed, encouraged, and long overdue.

Throughout our education and careers, we are encouraged as students and leaders to be independent; courageous; fearless; and, for the most part, traditional. These characteristics are often in conflict. Our traditional teaching framework is not facilitated through an entrepreneurial lens, and the business community chastises us as educators because our graduates lack the soft skills needed to advance in the workplace. Yet, we proffer soft skills as guiding principles toward teaching, learning, and success in the new paradigm of entrepreneurship. The entrepreneurial community college movement has given us permission to redefine the box, which for so many years has limited the progress of our colleges, our communities, and ourselves. Some of the guiding principles and questions cited in this book address the question, "What was the tipping point for you in your work?" in the following areas:

- Leadership matters: *Was it embedded in your culture, realistic, team-oriented, practical, and inspiring? What was the role of the CEOs? Have you replicated that kind of leadership in your own role?*
- Trust matters: *How have you developed trust? How have you connected with others?*
- Relationships matter: *How have you developed win-win relationships with individuals, groups, and teams? How do you best communicate with them and demonstrate how these relationships benefit them?*
- Ecosystems matter: *How have you mapped your assets and leveraged and built relationships?*
- Sustainability matters: *How have you facilitated this and provided effective training and support for your staff?*

Big Ideas

The contributors to this book have shared their individual and collective experiences and provided us with takeaways to remember and use as we continue this journey. Three of the major ideas reflected in the preceding chapters are particularly relevant in exploring the potential for a strong entrepreneurial focus in the community college:

1. The fundamental mission of the community college
2. Strengthening entrepreneurial pathways
3. Leading with an entrepreneurial mindset

The Fundamental Mission of the Community College

Pusser and Levin (2009) warn us that "each of the primary missions of community colleges faces a broad spectrum of challenges, made more complex by misapprehensions about the various roles of community colleges." With a focus on entrepreneurship in community colleges, this contemporary view is attributed to changing political policies, the focus on labor market outcomes, and leadership's inability to answer the question, *Do graduates find strong employment opportunity in well-paying jobs?* The role of entrepreneurship in job creation and economic growth is to stimulate competition and the economy. This capitalist purpose is consistent whether or not community colleges adopt an entrepreneurial mindset. New businesses bring disruption. They "challenge the existing market." Hakobyan (2017) notes:

> When a new business enters the local or global market, they begin to shake things up. Very few businesses open and try to be an exact replica of another company. Even if they have a similar mission statement and unique value propositions, they target a new niche or are expressing their brand differently.

Although this challenge may seem detrimental, disruption can also cause new jobs to open. Students with entrepreneurial training are much more adaptable and able to respond in a creative manner to changing market conditions than those who are not. Community college faculty and leadership have been able to reimagine and create environments where the infusion of an entrepreneurial mindset into certain courses—and, in some cases, the entire curriculum—is the norm. Infusing entrepreneurship into community colleges has spurred much enthusiasm but also much angst. Lackeus (2015) notes, "A myriad of effects has been stated to result from this, such as economic growth, job creation and increased societal resilience, but also individual growth, increased college engagement and improved equality" (p. 6).

However, moving a practice into policy has posed significant challenges despite the stated positive effects. Some institutional policymakers lack vision and see the proposed allocation of time and resources as diversions from the primary mission of teaching, learning, and jobs. Boards of trustees' fear of commercialism, impeding educational structures, and lack of definitional clarity are some of the challenges faculty and leadership have encountered when trying to infuse entrepreneurship into mainline community college education. The transformation of colleges requires a more basic understanding of twenty-first-century students and potential policy changes to directly align the goals of establishing an entrepreneurial mindset with the college's primary mission or goals. Additionally, such changes will allow increased collaboration with state and local policymakers regarding the possible impact on job creation and economic growth in the region.

"Re-imagining community colleges necessitates recognizing the connection between students who attend these institutions and the advanced learning and working environments beyond the community college" (Pusser & Levin, 2009). As we seek to bridge the gap between form and function, it may require that we think of community colleges as institutions with multiple missions and also imagine community colleges with organizational and governance structures that are aligned with multiple functions.

Strengthening Entrepreneurial Pathways

An initial step in ensuring strong entrepreneurial pathways is identifying the policies and priorities critical to helping colleges and states create more effective and efficient entrepreneurial education and workforce development systems. These systems should be designed with students in mind to prepare them for career success while increasing economic mobility and meeting workforce needs. Most of the policies and actions in the following list are, if not obvious, certainly topics that have been identified over time. And, of course, issues are going to vary from state to state and from college to college. I especially like the adage, "Policy doesn't keep up with practices," because we know that some colleges have moved ahead of implemented policy.

Critical Policies and Actions

1. There is inconsistency in *statewide transfer policies* from community colleges to baccalaureate institutions. Some states require the transfer of all credits in a degree, while others might transfer general education credits but not discipline credits. Some states legislate transfer policies; others don't. Intrastate transfer can be difficult, and interstate transfers even more so. *A national agenda for more seamless articulation/transfer agreements with an emphasis on entrepreneurial coursework would be helpful to students.*

2. There is no clear *articulation between noncredit programs/pathways to credit career pathways.* An example of this is in entrepreneurial apprenticeship programs, where the related instruction is offered for a noncredit/continuing education credential, with no formal arrangement for the learning that has taken place to be articulated with a related credit career pathway. *Dissemination and adoption of best practices in noncredit-to-credit pathway articulation would increase the value of noncredit learning and facilitate individuals advancing along a career pathway.*

3. A dichotomy remains between college transfer programs and career and entrepreneurial programs. *Given the need for flexible and nimble workers in the twenty-first century, the stature of entrepreneurial programs needs to be elevated.* High schools and colleges need to work together to ratchet up the importance of entrepreneurship programs. Strategies for enhancing the status of these programs include the following:
   - *Increase pathways and grow partnerships with secondary schools and Joint Technical Education Districts (JTEDs).* These partnerships can lead to greater funding streams through expansion of relationships between community colleges and secondary schools. They can

also develop greater and stronger pathways to increase dual and concurrent enrollment programs between the secondary system and JTEDs. These stronger entrepreneurial pathways need not be faculty based; instead, they can engage small business owners and operators throughout the students' educational pathway, from student selection, enrollment, internship, and apprenticeship, to the final course or program offering leading to student completion. In this approach, students learn about potential work possibilities throughout their program of study, and they know what skills and wages they will attain and master on their educational journey. These partnerships can also create greater opportunity for apprenticeships for students in nontraditional areas such as small business start-ups.

- *Develop 1+1 degree programs between community colleges and JTED technical schools and similar programs.* For example, the secondary-level JTEDs or technical schools could offer some of the general education classes while the community college offers the entrepreneurial classes. The degree is awarded by the community college but is conducted through the college's and the JTED's faculty.
- *Develop and increase state public policy and funding in entrepreneurial pathway development* in a linear, structured way that is aligned between the community colleges and secondary school pathways and is driven by small business needs.
- *Create sector strategies between employers, community colleges, and secondary schools* to develop programs that are responsive to needs of employers through state funding and the new Workforce Innovation and Opportunity Act structure. For example, the Maricopa County Community College District (MCCCD) has developed Business and Industry Leadership Teams (BILTs) in four main areas: manufacturing, information technology, health care, and advanced business services. These employer teams guide the district at the 20,000-foot level regarding larger trends and collaborative ways to serve specific industry clusters. The institutes, called MCCCD Centers for Excellence, are being developed with the support of these leadership teams.

Leading With an Entrepreneurial Mindset

Neil Kane (2016) proposes that the traditional career path is an anachronism.

Stats show 40 to 50 percent of students entering college in 2016 will be self-employed or will freelance at some point in their careers, according to a study commissioned by Intuit. The economy, students' desires and the world's expectations of students are all very different than what I faced when I graduated college.

Similarly, the personal career paths of many community college presidents and chancellors were not the paths intended by their undergraduate credentials, and, in some cases, were definitely not what these leaders expected. The Fourth Industrial Revolution, as described by author Bree Langemo in chapter 1, depicts the change in technology: Soft skills are actually more important than technical skills, and single technical skills may or may not create value in the future. She also states that the World Economic Forum anticipates that future workforce skills will focus on leadership, strategic and critical thinking, collaboration, problem-solving, and creativity over technical skills.

After graduating from college, my own career began with a position in a secondary school system. I worked for many years in the Illinois K through 12 public school system and expected to stay in K through 12 education for the rest of my career. When I answered the call to higher education, and specifically to community colleges, my prior experience did not adequately prepare me for this new world of work and my place in it. It did not prepare me for the challenges and opportunities of leading the MCCCD with an entrepreneurial mindset. However, my background as an elementary and secondary school business officer and college chief financial officer gave me a step up in the seat as chancellor.

I have learned that entrepreneurship is practiced each day as we seek alternative revenues or partnerships to advance teaching and learning. Entrepreneurship becomes a learned skill. Neil Kane (2016) maintains that when we educate faculty/staff and teach regarding the what, why, when and how of entrepreneurship, "the emphasis is on building skills, not starting businesses. . . . Rather the goal is about developing the inter-disciplinary skills that lead to the development of an entrepreneurial mindset."

My Maricopa Community College Learned Experience

I held the leadership positions of chancellor (2003–2016) and chief financial officer (1995–2003) for the MCCCD during a time of decreasing state funding. State resources began a steady decline in spring 1995 and culminated in March 2015 with the Arizona State Legislature withdrawing all funding for the district. Local and national news organizations reported the funding cut with dire headlines, including: "MCCCD loses all state funding" (Raburn, 2015); "Community colleges to lose all state funding under budget plan" (Olgin, 2015); and "Zeroed Out in Arizona" (Smith, 2015). Predictions about the drastic effects of this funding cut on the MCCCD were equally startling, with Board President Alfredo Gutierrez quoted as saying public education is "one organic system" and that the cuts to education "will do immense damage to our children at every level, including the community colleges" (Raburn, 2015). As chancellor, I noted in this article and other media reports that MCCCD had been dealing with decreases in state funding for several years and was prepared for this disinvestment in community college education. I explained that the district would be exploring options for reducing expenditures, reallocating resources, and identifying new revenue streams, and forecasted that, "We cannot cut our way out of this without having a totally different, new institution moving forward" (Raburn, 2015).

Media coverage of the district's plans for dealing with the withdrawal of state funds highlighted proposals for alternative revenue sources. For example, after I was interviewed by the *Phoenix Business Journal*, the ensuing article's headline read, "Maricopa Community Colleges Go Entrepreneurial to Replace Lost State Funds." The article and the interview provided an overview of losses in state funding and constraints on the community college district to find alternative sources of revenue (Gonzales, 2015). Dramatic reductions in funding—$68 million from 2008 to 2015—had led me, along with other college and community leaders, to rethink community college funding. With only "a mix of tuition, grants and property taxes to pay for [college] operations," I turned to entrepreneurial options. However, certain constitutional restrictions limited MCCCD's revenue-generating options, specifically legislation requiring property tax cuts if revenue from other fundraising sources reached certain levels (Gonzales, 2015).

My position on this legislation, as I said at the time, was that, "We're just asking for an opportunity. . . . If we can make money, don't limit us so we can actually replace some of the $68 million we have lost from the state of Arizona" (Gonzales, 2015). The major state universities had entrepreneurial revenue sources through patents and technology licensing, and I wanted MCCCD to have similar opportunities rather than relying on tuition increases. Allowing the Maricopa Community Colleges these opportunities would require only minor changes to legislation—or official interpretations of it—but these adjustments would have a major impact on the community college district's viability going forward. With 60% of the junior class at Arizona State University (ASU) made up of transfers from the Maricopa Community Colleges, our colleagues at ASU were supportive. Gonzales wrote about this support, quoting Maria Hesse, the vice provost of academic partnerships for ASU and a past president of Chandler-Gilbert Community College whose experience as an MCCCD president gave her a broad perspective on the synergistic relationship between the university, the 10 Maricopa Community Colleges, and the regional economy:

> As the funding environment in Arizona changes, we will do everything we can to sustain quality transfer programs, but limiting support for students in the Maricopa Community Colleges makes it more difficult for those students to transfer to, and graduate from, ASU as the master learners who will drive the future economy and strengthen our communities. (as quoted in Gonzales, 2015)

My thoughts about replacing the lost state revenue focused on the district's "economies of scale that can be used to provide management, technology, facilities rentals or other services to other colleges" (Gonzales, 2015). I used as one example Rio Learns, an online learning system developed by and for Rio Salado College, which could be licensed to institutions that lack the resources to produce or purchase their own. Another example, Maricopa Corporate College, provides customized training but could expand into other areas of business development. However, these and other ideas would not be allowed to replace the lost state funding unless the legislature changed the rules governing alternative revenue sources.

State Investment in Community Colleges: Arizona

Traditionally, *state investment* has been defined as funding, an accurate but narrow perspective implying that a total disinvestment could effectively represent a severance of the relationship between the state and its community colleges. At the very least, it suggests potentially unfunded mandates. Obviously, cuts first and foremost impact a college's ability to continue or increase service levels and other operational needs. However, another important aspect of state investment in education is support for the work of community colleges through removal of unnecessary regulatory or other legal constraints that limit their ability to serve in new ways and to secure new revenue streams. Arizona provides an instructive example of the changes emerging from the Great Recession.

The state's 10 organized districts and other provisional and tribal community colleges are the largest higher education provider in Arizona, with student populations significantly larger than the three public universities. As a result of the Great Recession, large cuts were made in state aid, not only to the Maricopa Community Colleges but also to community colleges across the state. The 2015 withdrawal of funding from MCCCD included the two largest districts, leading to a 100% loss of both capital and state aid for MCCCD and Pima Community College. In addition, the state rewrote statutes to exclude these two districts from receiving such aid in the future. Like MCCCD, Pima Community College adjusted by making spending cuts, minimizing new spending, and raising property taxes and tuition (the other two primary sources of funding), as appropriate and in ways designed to balance the need for more resources against the cost impact to property owners and students. At the same time, all of the state's community colleges sought and received relief from various legal requirements regarding reports, approvals, and other state-imposed limitations. None was more critical and significant than legislation passed in 2016 regarding the expenditure limitations of community colleges.

The expenditure limitation was Arizona's response to anti-tax concerns in the late 1970s, with the most well-known being California's Proposition 13. When voters in the state passed this referendum, it became part of the Arizona Constitution and established limits in the growth of budgets from revenues considered to be local. These local revenues are defined in the Constitution and include the major revenue source for general operating expenses, property taxes, operational state aid, and other resources. The expenditure limitation is a complex governing mechanism, but its calculation is quite simple: the budget for the base year of 1979–1980 is inflated by an inflation factor and expected full-time student equivalent, or FTSE. The 2016 legislation that was passed and signed into law addressed two major issues facing the state's community colleges:

1. It established methodologies for setting FTSE that allowed at least one community college to avoid implementing budget reductions to comply with limitation declines due to continuing enrollment losses. These cuts could have been crippling; they could have severely limited community colleges' ability to serve the numbers of students now attending or deliver the current suites of programs and courses.
2. It allowed revenues from entrepreneurial activities to be excluded from the limitation or to be used to offset expenditures. This opened the way for community colleges to engage in these activities without penalty.

The expenditure limitation and other regulatory reliefs were true victories and showed the state's commitment to investing in and supporting community colleges. Although funding cuts were not restored, these were significant accomplishments toward ensuring the viability of the community college system.

Although I had retired from the chancellor position when the 2016 legislation passed, the reduced limitations opened the door for the Maricopa Community Colleges to become more entrepreneurial and innovative in pursuing alternative revenue streams. For example, the Center for Entrepreneurial Innovation (CEI) houses the business incubation program and is located at GateWay Community College in Phoenix, Arizona. The CEI has taken the approach of executing a Royalty Payment Agreement with its graduating companies. The agreement calls for the company to make a payment to the CEI that is based on a percentage (or per unit cost) of sales. Currently, the center has one company under this type of agreement and anticipates two more soon. It also anticipates increased revenue to the college. Such an alternative revenue stream demonstrates a promising endeavor in promoting and understanding the bandwidth of possibilities for community colleges in the entrepreneurial space.

Closing Thoughts

The authors of the preceding chapters help clarify some basic tenets of entrepreneurship in the community college context. They focus on the value of all students learning to be entrepreneurial in preparation for dynamic careers in a rapidly changing world, and on the value of colleges—faculty, staff, and administrators—learning to be entrepreneurial in the face of dramatic shifts in the higher education landscape. The shared experiences and knowledge presented in this volume can inform community college practitioners, policy-makers, and other stakeholders seeking to build on the traditional missions of open access, workforce education, and community service to support regional economic development. With the lessons learned and takeaways provided by the authors, community college leaders can develop plans for creating an entrepreneurial mindset, starting with campus conversations around what this kind of forward-thinking movement would mean for the students and the institution.

Other steps might involve providing professional development and training in entrepreneurship for those who want to learn more, leading curriculum development, or engaging more intentionally in a broader conversation. With more background, a team can be better prepared to identify and connect with possible business, industry, and community partners and collaborators. Similarly, interested faculty can begin exploring how to integrate entrepreneurship into the curriculum. Ultimately, housing entrepreneurship on campus through makerspaces, incubators, professional networks, and similar types of innovation hubs, moves idea to action in a visible way, not only for the entrepreneurs who use the resources but also for students, faculty, and staff at the college who witness and help facilitate the process.

Our goal is to imbue through our words the spirit of entrepreneurship and to proffer that an entrepreneurial mindset can be learned. Hoover states in Chapter 6: "Generating pathways that connect programs to the community and to each other has become an ecosystem mantra for Northeast Ohio" (p. 86, this volume). Many of our communities know that we exist, but some do not know exactly what we do. Entrepreneurship is an expanding program and initiative in our colleges and serves as a pathway to our communities.

This movement is an opportunity to seek input and support to lead this change initiative and to serve as a catalyst for creating an entrepreneurial ecosystem. Giovannini emphasizes in chapter 3 that "entrepreneurial ecosystems that innovate and thrive can excel only when we leverage assets in new and creative ways and we structure strong support systems to help such ideas flourish" (p. 38, this volume). In chapter 7, Terrell and Kapp remind us that "creating and sustaining an entrepreneurial ecosystem and innovative economy cannot be achieved by a single organization or community" (p. 112, this volume). Political leaders and policymakers are looking for solutions to the ever-increasing costs of education and its need for funding. Entrepreneurship is a pathway to job creation and economic growth; however, the need to fund new mandates and to fully supplant revenues that are declining in college budgets remains a challenge.

References

Gonzales, A. (2015, July 27). Maricopa Community Colleges go entrepreneurial to replace lost state funds. *Phoenix Business Journal.* Available from www.bizjournals.com/phoenix/print-edition/2015/07/24/maricopa-community-colleges-go-entrepreneurial-to.html

Hakobyan, M. (2017, November 15). The role of entrepreneurship in job creation and economic growth [Web log post]. Available from www.huffingtonpost.com/margarita-hakobyan/the-role-of-entrepreneurs_b_12964394.html

Investopedia. (n.d.). *Neoliberalism.* Available from www.investopedia.com/terms/n/neoliberalism.asp

Kane, N. (2016, February 17). The entrepreneurial mindset. *360 Perspective.* Available from msutoday.msu.edu/360/2016/neil-kane-the-entrepreneurial-mindset/

Lackeus, M. (2015). *Entrepreneurship in education: What, why, when, how.* OECD. Available from www.oecd.org/cfe/leed/BGP_Entrepreneurship-in-Education.pdf

Olgin, A. (2015, March 5). Community colleges to lose all state funding under budget plan. *KJZZ*. Available from kjzz.org/content/109953/community-colleges -lose-all-state-funding-under-budget-plan

Pusser, B., & Levin, J. (2009, December 8). Re-imaging community colleges in the 21st century. *Center for American Progress*. Available from www.americanprogress.org/ issues/economy/reports/2009/12/08/7083/re-imagining-community-colleges-in-the-21st-century/

Raburn, J. (2015, April 2). MCCCD loses all state funding. *Northeast Valley News*. Available from nevalleynews.org/2832/news/mcccd-loses-all-state-funding

Smith, A. A. (2015, March 12). Zeroed out in Arizona. *Inside Higher Ed*. Available from www.insidehighered.com/news/2015/03/12/arizona-unprecedented-defunding-community-colleges

Zecher Sutton, B. (2016, June 20). Higher education's public purpose [Web log post]. Available from www.aacu.org/leap/liberal-education-nation-blog/higher-educations-public-purpose

Threw preceding chapters and pages of this book are replete with information and perspectives critical to meeting and shaping the future of the community college sector. A recurrent theme, and now an imperative, is the reality that if we are to meet the challenges of the second century of the community college movement, we must begin to think and behave very differently. We should start with what we think we know now, remember what we've forgotten, and be comfortable with what we don't know about the future. In short, to navigate successfully to meet the needs of students and communities, we must adopt an entrepreneurial mindset—letting our passion dictate our direction while exercising moral courage and risk-taking to shift the curve of decision-making by rejecting the status quo.

To meet and conquer our challenges we must infuse our leadership with entrepreneurial principles. Saras Sarasvathy, professor at the University of Virginia's Darden Graduate School of Business Administration, has studied the behaviors and traits of entrepreneurs, and these habits can be directly applied to how community college leaders can rise to meet the challenges of the future.

The "bird-in-the-hand" principle allows leaders to begin with assessing assets and having resources at the ready to re-establish the starting line for effecting real change. Using the "affordable-loss" principle creates the ground on which leaders can stake assets to invest in change by accepting that not all risk capital yields results. By applying the "crazy quilt" principle, community college leaders can pursue new and different public/private partnerships to bring resources and expertise to bear on solving problems that colleges cannot solve alone. Using all available "lemons" allows leaders to maximize return on investment (ROI) and scalability in ways that unleash higher returns from existing resources and assets. And finally, by being the "pilot in the plane," leaders become more directly engaged in moving the institution closer to the horizon by, in effect, turning off the autopilot that too frequently characterizes colleges' behaviors and the resistance to change.

In short, applying entrepreneurial principles allows leaders to approach decision-making with much more intentionality and purpose, shifting the culture to embracing risk-taking and using real data to break down the status quo. Leaders must master new cultural and experiential competencies and become cocreators and lead by example, just as entrepreneurs do. There are no simple algorithms to master entrepreneurship—the science of entrepreneurship can be described and disseminated. The art of entrepreneurship is in the doing—the relentless passion. In the words of George Bernard Shaw's *Back to Methuselah*: "You see things; you say, 'Why?' But I dream things that never were; and I say 'Why not?'" Now is the time for doing. It is time to become habitual entrepreneurial community college leaders.

J. Noah Brown
President and CEO,
Association of Community College Trustees;
Former Member, NACCE Board of Directors

Reference

Shaw, G. B. (1922/2011). *Back to Methuselah*. Overland Park, KS: Digireads.com Publishing.

NACCE, A Retrospective

Rebecca A. Corbin and Ron Thomas

Andy Scibelli was ahead of his time in starting a movement rooted in entrepreneurial leadership and teaching. As president of Springfield Technical Community College (STCC) for 21 years, he was an innovative and inspirational leader, committed to helping students succeed and grow the Springfield economy. He had an entrepreneurial mindset marked by resourcefulness and persistence in identifying opportunities, building coalitions, and making projects happen. Scibelli believed a new college program could help entrepreneurs launch or grow their businesses and overcome the traditionally high failure rates. Developing an entrepreneurial mindset was a critical bridge for building a better tomorrow. Scibelli's idea for an entrepreneurship program at STCC would ignite a national movement that led to the creation of National Association for Community College Entrepreneurship (NACCE).

In 1995, Scibelli commissioned a feasibility study for a potential entrepreneurship program. The study confirmed that a small business incubator aligned with the expertise of the college could foster business growth in the region. As a result of the study, STCC made the decision to move forward with an entrepreneurship program.

After the feasibility study was completed, the college enlisted the help of two consultants to help move the entrepreneurship program forward: Tommy Goodrow and Steve Spinelli. Goodrow, an entrepreneur and consultant, was later hired as vice president of the college. Spinelli was cofounder of Jiffy Lube International, former director of the Arthur M. Blank Center for Entrepreneurship at Babson College, and is currently chancellor emeritus of Thomas Jefferson University. Goodrow and Spinelli met with staff, community, and business leaders to develop a framework for the entrepreneurship program.

With the closure of the Springfield Armory next to STCC in 1965, the college had additional facilities to house the entrepreneurship program, though significant renovation was needed. Seeking funding for the renovation, the college recruited a fund-raising team led by Gail Carberry, vice president of institutional advancement at STCC. She and her team worked with community leaders and advisory boards to raise funds for the retrofit and move the entrepreneurship program into its new home.

This "can-do" mindset reaped huge dividends for STCC. The college was awarded a prestigious $3 million National Science Foundation grant to create the Northeast Center for Telecommunications Technology and open the STCC Technology Park adjacent to the college. In an interview with *Business West*, STCC executive vice president John Dunn, said, "[Scibelli] created an environment that has not only inspired creativity, but also a strong sense of commitment to the institution" (O'Brien, 1998).

The team raised more than $3 million, which included a $990,000 Economic Development Administration grant to complete the Entrepreneurial Institute in 1999. The institute provided educational programming and included a student incubator, a college, a high school, and K through 8 entrepreneurship educational programs.

From the widespread interest drawn by the Entrepreneurial Institute grew the idea of a national membership organization, the National Association for Community College Entrepreneurship. Wisely, Scibelli chose entrepreneurial community college leaders to serve as the founding directors for NACCE. Goodrow was named chairman with founding directors Ron Thomas, Kevin Drumm, Donald Schoening, and Sheila Ortego.

Going National

STCC had been sharing its entrepreneurship stories of success and failure with hundreds of people who wanted to visit the campus and see the creative enterprise. Others who could not make the journey to Springfield wanted to talk on the phone. Clearly, there was a growing interest among community colleges about the importance of entrepreneurship and a need for a national association that would support and grow this interest.

Launching any type of national organization is a daunting task. However, beginning in 2002, Goodrow and his team put in the work to form NACCE. S. Prestley Blake, cofounder of the Friendly Ice Cream Corporation in 1935 and a longtime supporter of STCC, earmarked a $100,000 gift to create the first NACCE conference in October 2003. Additional support for the conference was provided by the Coleman Foundation, the Ewing Marion Kauffman Foundation, and in-kind support from STCC. A total of 150 people attended NACCE's first annual conference.

The Growing Years

With an early, sizable financial investment from the Coleman Foundation in 2003, NACCE extended its national impact by funding entrepreneurship projects at community colleges across the country. This milestone solidified NACCE as a leading voice on the value of community college entrepreneurship education. Diane Sabato, a longtime advocate of NACCE and professor of business at STCC, credits NACCE with making entrepreneurship part of the national conversation (NACCE, 2017). And, as more community colleges launched entrepreneurship programs, NACCE membership grew, and NACCE and business communities across the country forged new partnerships in increasing numbers. By 2011, the organization's rising profile prompted an invitation from the White House to participate in President Barack Obama's public/private Startup America initiative.

NACCE Effectuates to Pivot and Expand

Heather Van Sickle served as NACCE's president from 2005 until 2015. During her tenure, the Coleman Foundation played a vital role in helping NACCE grow and develop by providing $2 million in funding between 2003 and 2015. Many of these funds were granted to NACCE member colleges for initiatives presented in a competition at NACCE's annual conference.

When Van Sickle left NACCE and was replaced by Rebecca Corbin, the Coleman Foundation grant concluded, ushering in a new organizational model based on creating revenue streams with a variety of funders and members. This model proved to be effective. By diversifying funding streams and seizing new opportunities that could be implemented as community of practice projects, NACCE grew financially, maintaining a small staff of five with key consultants and committed volunteer members who were supported by a strong and active governing board.

Notably, NACCE followed the advice it delivered to its member colleges: identify strengths and attributes in your community, work with local industries and businesses, and cocreate in concert with nearby community colleges and other institutions. Finding new, like-minded partners for revenue-shared agreements and engaging faculty and administrators in member colleges to engage in creating new resources to spur entrepreneurial teaching and leadership, strengthened NACCE's effectiveness and ability to build a reserve for the future. It also allowed NACCE to show impact in its reach and in its work, which were propelled by two major initiatives—ecosystem mapping and the *Presidents for Entrepreneurship Pledge* (*PFEP*).

Ecosystem Mapping

Mapping assets and leveraging opportunity—in a community or on an ecosystem basis—is the foundation for what Saras Sarasvathy, professor at the University of Virginia's Darden Graduate School of Business Administration, terms the *bird-in-hand principle* for entrepreneurs. Entrepreneurs must start with their means, which can be grouped into three categories: *who I am*—my traits, tastes and abilities; *what I know*—my education, training, expertise, and experience; and *who I know*—my social and professional networks (Corbin & Schulz, 2018).

In January 2015, during NACCE's own rebuilding process, one important "bird-in-hand" asset came in the form of a federal grant for $99,342 from the Appalachian Regional Commission (ARC). The grant was matched by NACCE with $44,889. These assets helped NACCE support technical assistance training in the area of innovation in entrepreneurship among 11 Appalachian community colleges in poverty-distressed areas. ARC funds and cost-sharing were used for personnel, travel, contractual, and online training expenses.

Van Sickle had forged NACCE's relationship with ARC, and when she left, Corbin and Amy Schulz (a staff member and consultant for NACCE in 2016 and 2017) worked together to encourage the colleges to step outside their comfort zones and work together to identify their "bird-in-hand" assets and ways they could collaborate to make an impact in the area of economic development and job creation. The creative process unleashed some projects that continue to grow and produce revenue today.

One example is Big Sandy Community and Technical College (BSCTC) in Eastern Kentucky. BSCTC successfully leveraged other funding sources and stakeholders to create an American Metal Works Incubator, host a regional symposium on entrepreneurship, and expand its course offerings (Corbin & Schulz, 2017). The entrepreneurial activity continued at BSCTC in 2018 with the production and sales of an entrepreneurial coloring book aimed at getting primary school-age children interested in entrepreneurship.

Ecosystem mapping is a valuable tool, which Corbin and Schulz (2017) made the case for when they presented a paper at the International Society of Academic Maker Spaces (ISAM) that made the following argument:

> Today's complex problems require a systems approach, which incorporates diverse stakeholders and holistic solutions. By mapping an ecosystem of

stakeholders within the system, the complexity of players and relationships can be visually decoded for participants. Mapping an ecosystem involves identifying members of the ecosystem and making relational connections. The map itself is merely a tool to be utilized to develop key relationships, leverage physical and social capital, and plan a strategy to meet the objectives of the ecosystem. (Auerswald, 2015)

The ARC project that was organized as a community of practice in Table A.1 identified mentor colleges as those further along in the entrepreneurial journey and partner colleges as those that aspired to be more entrepreneurial in leadership and teaching approaches in the community and in the classroom.

NACCE's work with these 11 community colleges to create an ecosystem map of their communities has continued. With a 2017–2018 funded grant through the ARC, NACCE is working with 6 community colleges in Eastern Kentucky to train 72 faculty in the CORE curriculum and provide them with entrepreneurial coaching and support. In mapping these means or assets across an ecosystem, communities have not just assembled them, but also discovered new ones. Certain skills essential to traditional industries, for instance, have application to new technology. In West Virginia, skilled labor in old-school manufacturing has proven to be an advantage for advanced manufacturing. Eastern West Virginia Community and Technical College has transformed agricultural expertise into AgTech proficiency (Corbin & Schulz, 2018).

TABLE A.1
NACCE Appalachian Community of Practice

Mentor and Partner Colleges	State
Garrett College	MD
Northeast State Community College	TN
Patrick Henry Community College	VA
Eastern West Virginia Community & Technical College	WV
Hazard Community & Technical College	KY
Big Sandy Community & Technical College	KY
Southeast Kentucky Community & Technical College	KY
Southern West Virginia Community & Technical College	WV
Somerset Community & Technical College	KY
Ashland Community & Technical College	KY
Roane State Community College	TN

With entrepreneurship being so closely linked with Silicon Valley, it may seem counterintuitive that California is learning how to build entrepreneurial ecosystems from Appalachia, but it is. These 11 community colleges in Appalachia that created ecosystem maps with a first-generation open source tool, Mindmeister, have led to a larger ecosystem-building project in California. Both efforts can inform communities nationwide. Every community college—rural, urban, or suburban—can begin taking entrepreneurial steps. Identifying local entrepreneurs to speak at a college event or participate as judges in pitch competitions can be the start of growing entrepreneurial events. (Corbin & Schulz, 2018)

The Presidents for Entrepreneurship Pledge

When economic gears shifted from plentitude and growth during the 1990s to a paucity of economic opportunity from 2000 to 2010, community colleges were plunged into new economic realties. Reduced budgets, higher accountability standards, and the waning number of professionals prepared for community college leadership created a crisis for community colleges. A new leadership model was needed for community college leaders to meet these challenges, and in response, NACCE unveiled the *PFEP* in 2011 (see Figure A.1).

The initiative was designed to assist community college presidents in advancing entrepreneurship in their communities and creating a culture of entrepreneurship on their campuses. Van Sickle provided the staff leadership for this initiative. The *PFEP* model was based on five commitments community college presidents were asked to make based on successful entrepreneurship activities reported from NACCE members.

The five commitments are:

1. Form teams to focus on entrepreneurship
2. Connect with entrepreneurs in the community
3. Collaborate with industry in your region
4. Focus on business and job creation
5. Share stories through events and the media

Fortunately, community college leaders have a long history of innovation and the ability to seek opportunities to better serve their colleges and communities, and college leaders across the country embraced the *PFEP*. By the end of 2017, 164 presidents of community colleges in 37 states had signed the pledge.

The cogency of the pledge was tested by an independent survey, the *PFEP* Validation Report, which was funded by the Coleman Foundation in 2015. With an 83% completion rate, the assessment results clearly demonstrated that the *PFEP* had and continues to have a significant impact in the way community colleges act and perceive themselves as entrepreneurially minded institutions. The question for college leaders thus became "How to build on the commitment colleges had already made to the *PFEP*?" To explore this query, community college presidents met in April 2015 at the 95th annual meeting of the American Association of Community Colleges (AACC). During that event, NACCE hosted a breakfast (Figure A.2) in which 20 community college presidents gathered to learn about the results of the *PFEP* assessment, and to focus on three areas of challenge and how entrepreneurship could help them meet these challenges (People Talent Solutions, 2014).

The first challenge identified was enrollment. Ideas for meeting this challenge included developing a model program for a two-year certificate, focusing on burgeoning academic areas like bio-science, and showing colleges how to create start-up incubators. The second challenge identified was retention and the completion agenda. The ideas discussed here focused on fostering best practice alignment with high schools, teaching the entrepreneurial mindset as part of student success in high school and college, and engaging the business community to increase work-based learning experiences and internships. The third challenge centered on budget and revenue issues, and the presidents engaged in creative discussions about alternate revenue sources, including developing makerspaces and incubators and raising private funds to support college ventures.

These questions served as guideposts to lingering issues that NACCE's board members and the newly appointed president and CEO Rebecca Corbin would begin to focus on in 2015 and beyond (Corbin, 2015).

Figure A.1. NACCE's Presidents for Entrepreneurship Pledge.

Figure A.2. The 2015 AACC breakfast.

Throughout its existence, NACCE experimented with adding entrepreneurs and faculty to its board of directors. However, by 2015, the NACCE board committed to maintaining its role in governance and supporting the president and CEO and staff in conducting the organization's daily work.

The organization formed its board structure into 13 community college presidents representing all geographic regions in the United States, with an additional director from a Canadian college and senior leaders from the AACC and the Association of Community College Trustees (ACCT).

In 2016, NACCE was able to get a seat at the table through invitations to Demo Day, the TechHire Initiative, and other White House–sponsored events geared to spur entrepreneurship (National Association for Community College Entrepreneurship, 2018). In 2017, NACCE granted over $500,000 to 13 community colleges to engage in entrepreneurial projects. Over $3 million was secured for 2018 to 2020 to be re-granted through NACCE to community colleges. Technical assistance support enabled NACCE to help foster the creation of 24 makerspaces in California and form effective partnerships between K through 12 and community college partners in Appalachia. This work continues.

After 16 years of incredible growth, NACCE's membership includes 300-plus colleges in the United States and abroad. Among its members are 2,000 faculty, staff, administrators, and presidents who serve 3 million students throughout North America. Globally, NACCE has extended its partnerships to a university in China and is sharing entrepreneurial curriculum and community support systems for entrepreneurship with college leaders throughout the world.

Takeaways

- Successful leaders must have an entrepreneurial mindset.
- Learn how to solve a problem with your assets and leverage strengths of other partners.
- Trust is key to successful change. Know how to build trust in your planning process.
- Timing for any project plays a critical role in the successful launch.
- The key to success is building an ecosystem of support. Start by mapping yours.
- New programs must be validated and evaluated to ensure success.
- Communicate early and often with stakeholders and those you're serving.

References

Auerswald, P. (2015, October). *Enabling entrepreneurial ecosystems: Insights from ecology to inform effective entrepreneurship policy.* Kauffman Foundation Research Series on City, Metro, and Regional Entrepreneurship, Kansas City, MO.

Corbin, R. (2015). *Generating revenue in Southern New Jersey community colleges: An examination of entrepreneurship, philanthropy, and workforce development practices* (Published dissertation No. 3732544). Wilmington University, Wilmington, DE.

Corbin, R., & Schulz, A. (2017, September 25). *Evolution of education ecosystems applied to innovation education.* Paper presented at the International Society of Academic Makerspaces, Case Western Reserve University, Cleveland, OH.

Corbin, R., & Schulz, A. (2018, February). How ecosystem mapping by colleges can transform struggling communities. *Education Dive.* Available from https://www.educationdive.com/news/how-ecosystem-mapping-by-colleges-can-help-transform-struggling-communities/517830/

National Association for Community College Entrepreneurship. (2018). *2017 annual report of the National Association for Community College Entrepreneurship.* Available from https://cdn.ymaws.com/nacce.site-ym.com/resource/resmgr/Annual_Report_2017.PDF

O'Brien, G. (1998, September). The small community college has grown into a national leader. *Business West, 14*, 14–16.

People Talent Solutions. (2014). *Presidents for entrepreneurship validation summary report.* Available from http://c.ymcdn.com/sites/www.nacce.com/resource/resmgr/PFE/Validation_Report_Coleman_Fo.pdf?hhSearchTerms=%22Presidents+and+Entrepreneurship+and+Pledge+and+Validation%22)

ABOUT THE CONTRIBUTORS

Rebecca A. Corbin has served in leadership roles in the community college system for the past decade, as president and chief executive officer of the National Association for Community College Entrepreneurship, and as vice president of institutional advancement and executive director of the Foundation for Rowan College at Burlington County in New Jersey. Her passion is fund-raising and sharing thought leadership and practical applications for infusing entrepreneurship on campus and in communities by writing articles and presenting at national and international conferences. She has an EdD in innovation and organizational leadership from Wilmington University in Delaware, an MA in public administration from the University of Akron, and a BA from Kent State University.

Eugene Giovannini serves as chancellor for the Tarrant County College District, an institution serving nearly 100,000 students in the Dallas–Fort Worth area. He has more than 30 years of professional experience at community colleges, including his role as founding president of Maricopa Corporate College in Scottsdale, Arizona, and 11 years as president of GateWay Community College in Phoenix. Giovannini has served as the board chair for the National Association for Community College Entrepreneurship and as a board member of the American Association of Community Colleges. He has extensive involvement with workforce and economic development efforts and has a passion for "doing the right things right." Giovannini believes strongly in the power of entrepreneurial ecosystems and their impact on communities. He has a BA and an MA in business education from Bloomsburg University and an EdD in community college education from Virginia Polytechnic Institute and State University.

Rufus Glasper is president and CEO of the League for Innovation in the Community College, an international nonprofit organization with a mission to cultivate innovation in the community college environment in a continuing effort to advance the community college field and make a positive difference for students and communities. Glasper, chancellor emeritus of the Maricopa Community Colleges, served as chancellor from May 2003 through February 2016, and previously held district leadership positions for two decades. He earned a BA in business administration from Luther

College, Decorah, Iowa, and an MA and advanced degrees in school business administration from Northern Illinois University. He received a PhD in higher education finance from the University of Arizona.

Andrew Gold is an assistant professor of entrepreneurship and business administration at Hillsborough Community College (HCC) in Tampa, Florida, and an adjunct faculty member at the University of Tampa, and the University of South Florida, where he teaches in the MBA programs. Gold has over 25 years of experience as an entrepreneur, starting several businesses over that period with a focus on social entrepreneurship. He earned his BA in psychology from the State University of New York–Oswego, his MA in international business from Manhattanville College, and his PhD in business administration from Northcentral University.

Carrie Henderson serves as the executive vice chancellor of the Florida College System. In this role, she provides leadership over academic and student affairs, research and analytics, and financial policy. Prior to this position, Henderson served as associate vice president for institutional effectiveness and accreditation at Florida State College at Jacksonville and as associate director of programs at Achieving the Dream, Inc. Her interests and experience include institutional effectiveness, strategic planning, resource development, and institutional research. Henderson holds a PhD in higher education administration, a graduate certificate in institutional research from Florida State University, an MA in public administration from the University of North Carolina at Chapel Hill, and a BA in history and political science from the University of Central Florida.

Deborah Hoover has served as president and CEO of Burton D. Morgan Foundation, a philanthropic champion of the entrepreneurial spirit based in Northeast Ohio, for the last decade. Morgan Foundation seeks to build the entrepreneurial mindset in children, teens, and college students through educational and experiential opportunities that target problem-solving and innovation skills. For adult entrepreneurs, the foundation works with its ecosystem partners to provide new ventures and their founders with ready access to knowledge, mentors, and financing. Hoover has a BA from Williams College, an MA from the University of Chicago, and a JD from George Washington University.

Joe Kapp has served as the entrepreneur in residence at Eastern West Virginia Community and Technical College since 2013. A serial entrepreneur, he started and sold his first business, a video production company, while still in college. Since that time he has consulted to Fortune 500 companies and has started numerous successful ventures and nonprofits. In 2015, Kapp was invited to the White House to participate in the first "Demo Day," which showcased the talents of innovators and entrepreneurs from across the country. The following year, he was appointed by U.S. Secretary of Commerce, Penny Pritzker, to serve on the National Advisory Council on Innovation and Entrepreneurship (NACIE). In 2017, Kapp cofounded the National Center for Resource Development to help foundations, nonprofits, and higher education institutions achieve greater impact by more effectively executing their missions. Kapp was recently profiled by the *Washington Post Sunday Magazine* for his work in entrepreneurship in rural communities. He has a BA from Florida State University and an MA in government administration from the University of Pennsylvania.

Mary Beth Kerly has over 18 years of community college experience. She earned her BA in marketing and her MBA from Goldey-Beacom College in Wilmington, Delaware. She currently serves as a professor of business and entrepreneurship at Hillsborough Community College (HCC) in Tampa, Florida, and an adjunct professor for management and strategy at the University of Tampa. In 2015, Andrew Gold and Kerly cofounded e2Venture, a consulting business that provides entrepreneurial mindset training services to organizations, educators, and at-risk youth. They have successfully developed and redesigned 4 academic degree and certificate programs, launched 10 new community events supporting entrepreneurship, cultivated over 40 new partnerships to support college programming, and secured over $2 million in grants and sponsorships in partnership with HCC.

Bree Langemo has spent more than a decade as a community college faculty member, chair, and dean. An accountant and attorney, she is also the former president of the Entrepreneurial Learning Initiative (ELI), where she led with a focus on developing high impact partnerships with academic, government, profit, and nonprofit organizations around the world to empower their constituents with an entrepreneurial mind set. She led the development of ELI's Ice House Student Success program and was featured in the *Huffington Post* for pioneering Ice House as a student success course. She is the founding member and board chair for uCodeGirl, a nonprofit focused on developing computing and entrepreneurial skills in young girls to inspire them in the technology careers of the future. She earned her BA in accounting from Minnesota State University-Moorhead and a JD from Ohio Northern University College of Law.

Christopher Mullin is an expert in the areas of higher education policy, research, and practice having served as the director of Strong Start to Finish, executive vice chancellor of the Florida College System, assistant vice chancellor for Policy and Research at the State University System of Florida, and the program director of policy analysis for the American Association of Community Colleges (AACC) in Washington DC. In all capacities, his work has focused on empowering students and communities to maximize their full potential. He is a prolific writer, having coauthored books, journal articles, policy briefs, and various other publications that have been cited in *The Wall Street Journal, The Chronicle of Higher Education, Inside Higher Education*, and *EdWeek,* among others. Mullin earned his PhD in higher education administration, as well as his BA, from the University of Florida. He earned his MEd from Teachers College of Columbia University.

Madeline M. Pumariega is the former chancellor of the 28 colleges that make up the Florida College System, which serves more than 800,000 students. Recognized among the top college systems in the nation, the Florida College System is committed to maintaining the highest quality programs to meet Florida's growing workforce needs and to make sure college is accessible and affordable. Appointed as the first female and Hispanic chancellor in August 2015, Pumariega has worked to build on the successes of the Florida College System. A product of the college system herself, Pumariega began her academic career at Miami Dade College and returned to the college where she spent 20 years growing her career, culminating as president of the Wolfson campus. Before becoming chancellor, Pumariega served as president of Take Stock in Children, a statewide nonprofit organization focused on breaking the cycle of poverty through education. Pumariega is a member of the Florida Prepaid College Board, Higher Education Coordinating Council, and Florida Council of 100. She has an MEd from Florida Atlantic University and a PhD in community college leadership from Barry University.

Steven Tello serves as vice provost for innovation and workforce development at UMass Lowell. In this position Tello oversees the development and growth of UMass Lowell's graduate programs, online education programs, and international partnerships. Tello has been instrumental in the rapid growth of the M2D2 and Innovation Hub business incubators, student DifferenceMaker program, River Hawk Venture Fund, and the Deshpande Symposium on Innovation and Entrepreneurship. He is a tenured associate professor in the Manning School of Business, where he founded the school's undergraduate and graduate entrepreneurship programs. He has an MA in education from Cambridge College, an MBA from the University of Massachusetts at Amherst, and an EdD in educational leadership from the University of Massachusetts at Lowell.

Charles Terrell, dubbed the "mustachioed, tattooed community college president" by *Washington Post Magazine*, has served as president of Eastern West Virginia Community and Technical College (Eastern) in Moorefield, West Virginia, for eight years. Terrell's experience encompasses student services, college counseling, teaching, and workforce development. In 2012, he was one of the first community college presidents in the country to sign NACCE's *Presidents for Entrepreneurship Pledge*, thereby making a commitment to create an entrepreneurial culture at Eastern and an entrepreneurial ecosystem in the Potomac Highlands of West Virginia. In 2016, he was named Entrepreneurial President of the Year by NACCE. Terrell has a BA from East Carolina University, an MA in community and college counseling from Longwood University, and a PhD in education from Virginia Commonwealth University.

Ron Thomas served for 17 years as president of two-year colleges. He joined the National Association for Community College Entrepreneurship (NACCE) in 2003, serving as a board member and chairman for two years. During his tenure as chairman, Thomas was instrumental in the launch of the *Presidents for Entrepreneurship Pledge* in 2011. His passion for entrepreneurship includes writing articles, presenting at national conferences, and working to create entrepreneurship programs and opportunities. He has a PhD from Southern Illinois University–Carbondale, an MA from Southern Illinois University–Edwardsville, and a BA from Truman State University.

Van Ton-Quinlivan is vice chancellor of workforce and digital futures for the California Community Colleges, composed of 115 colleges. Ton-Quinlivan's leadership focus is Doing What MATTERS for Jobs and the Economy (doingwhatMATTERS.cccco.edu) with the goal of improving workforce outcomes for California's 2.1 million community college students and fueling strong regional economies. She was named a White House Champion of Change in 2013 for her distinguished career in industry, education, and community service and, in 2017, received the statewide California Steward Leader Award, selected for her significant contributions to align public, private, and civic sector leaders to promote economic and social progress in all regions of the state. She is vice chair of the National Skills Coalition, cochair of the Workforce Action Team of the California Economic Summit and serves on the California Council on Science and Technology. Ton-Quinlivan holds degrees from the Stanford Graduate School of Business, Stanford Graduate School of Education, and Georgetown University.

Doan Winkel is the John J. Kahl Sr. Chair in Entrepreneurship and director of The Edward M. Muldoon Center for Entrepreneurship at John Carroll University. In this role, Winkel is developing the next frontier in university-based entrepreneurship curriculum and programming. He is the founder and director of the Entrepreneurship Education Project, which gathers data from nearly 20,000 college students from 400-plus universities across 70-plus countries to better understand how to teach entrepreneurship. Winkel cofounded internrocket.com, Legacy Out Loud, and The BuildHers to help young people discover and pursue their passion as a career path. He also cofounded TeachingEntrepreneurship.org, an experiential entrepreneurship curriculum used by university students around the world. He is the senior vice president of Programming of the United States Association for Small Business and Entrepreneurship, the editor-in-chief of the *Experiential Entrepreneurship Exercises Journal*, and a contributing editor of *Entrepreneurship Education & Pedagogy*. Winkel received his MBA from Colorado State University and his PhD in Organizational Behavior and Entrepreneurship from the University of Wisconsin–Milwaukee.

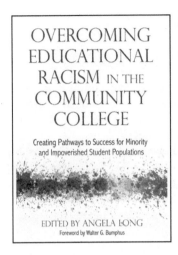

OVERCOMING
EDUCATIONAL
RACISM IN THE
COMMUNITY
COLLEGE

Creating Pathways to Success for Minority
and Impoverished Student Populations

EDITED BY ANGELA LONG
Foreword by Walter G. Bumphus

Overcoming Educational Racism in the Community College

Creating Pathways to Success for Minority and Impoverished Student Populations

Edited by Angela Long

Foreword by Walter G. Bumphus

"What an incredible collection of research, best practices, and leaders on the most important topic of our nation—how to address inequity caused by educational racism. Community colleges are uniquely positioned to provide the opportunity for consciousness and job skills for those most underserved. As was the aim of the Obama administration, improving the graduation rates from community colleges—where the majority of first generation, African American, Latino, Native American, and working class students attend—is the only way to educate our nation and be, once again, the most educated country."—*José A. Rico, Former Executive Director, White House Initiative on Educational Excellence for Hispanics*

"Persistent equity gaps threaten the future of our society, and there is only one institution in America that has the potential to close them. *Overcoming Educational Racism in the Community College* draws on the perspectives of our best researchers and leaders to remind us of the urgency of the problems and to identify promising practices that can make a difference." —*Dr. George Boggs, President & CEO Emeritus, American Association of Community Colleges*

22883 Quicksilver Drive
Sterling, VA 20166-2019

Subscribe to our e-mail alerts: www.Styluspub.com